The Love that Remains

10

SUSAN
FRANCIS

The Love that Remains

ALLEN&UNWIN
SYDNEY·MELBOURNE·AUCKLAND·LONDON

Allen & Unwin
83 Alexander Street
Crows Nest NSW 2065
Australia
Phone:(61 2) 8425 0100
Email:info@allenandunwin.com
Web:www.allenandunwin.com

 A catalogue record for this
book is available from the
National Library of Australia

ISBN 978 1 76087 672 2

Internal design by Post Pre-press Group
Set in 12/17 pt Bembo by Post Pre-press Group, Australia
Printed and bound in Australia by Griffin Press, part of Ovato

10 9 8 7 6 5 4 3 2 1

 The paper in this book is FSC® certified.
FSC® promotes environmentally responsible,
socially beneficial and economically viable
management of the world's forests.

'What's past is prologue.'

William Shakespeare

For Di, because she kept faith.
And for my son, Jonno, who saved me.

. . . Here's the story I promised I would tell you Wayne—about Aristophanes and his theory explaining love.

He believed that we were created as two individuals, attached back to back. Our separate faces looked in opposite directions, we shared four arms and four legs and we spent our beautiful days cartwheeling around the world without thought.

Then we became too happy for our own good: we assumed too much. The attempt to ascend to heaven was a step too far—even happiness had boundaries.

The gods took their revenge. They cleaved the one of us into two. And now?

Now we're forever destined to spend our life roaming the world—searching for our soulmate: the other half of our true self.

Because it's the only way we can be whole again . . .

Prologue

Granada, Spain, January 2015

I HAVE A CLEAR MEMORY of Wayne throwing his arm about my shoulders, the weight of him fixing me where I stood. Despite the climb, I couldn't stop shivering, so he rubbed my hands, tried to warm me up. Easiest lesson I learnt that year was how bitter Spain is in wintertime.

Later, after hoisting my bags across a frozen puddle of water, I clambered after my husband as best I could. Till around another corner we emerged into weak sunlight, choosing a courtyard—dandelions sprouting out of cracked cement—in which to take a rest. Where we wiped cold noses and watched our breath freeze in front of our faces.

Yet even with the weather, the exhaustion, and a niggling instinct that whispered to me that we'd lost our way—on that afternoon, wrapped in each other's arms, we laughed into the silence. Even as we struggled to catch our breath, even as he kissed me full on the lips, one realisation was clear: we'd made it—this was Granada!

Two feral cats arched on a window ledge, glowered at us, ready for flight. The larger one yowled and disappeared in an explosion of fur. I shivered, and tucked my hands deep into my duffle coat.

1

The echo of boots knocking against stone made me glance up. A wizened old man had appeared out of nowhere, his back bent in half from balancing a stack of firewood. The sun was low behind us and shadows lengthened the cobblestone path ahead, so we followed the Spaniard up the rise like he was the Pied Piper.

The passageway narrowed and I stretched my arms out, finger-tips trailing the white walls of the rustic villas lined up side-by-side, next to the path. We were climbing through the original Arab quarter, famed for its labyrinth of stone corridors. Directly above us loomed the Alhambra: a castle created from red clay, built by the Muslims who dominated Andalusia during the early Middle Ages. I caught a glimpse of the snow-covered Sierra Nevada mountain range in the distance, sensed as much as saw the splendour—and why the surrounding streets had been heritage listed. I listened to water splashing in the streams and spilling from the palace gardens.

But, bumping my suitcase over the stones, lungs burning, I couldn't keep up. I lagged behind Wayne. Lagged even further behind the Spaniard. Stumbling under a medieval archway, I watched my husband from a distance as he wrestled his bags up another steep ascent. The old Andalusian man had already vanished.

I told myself it was only for a moment. Leant back against a wrought-iron gate. Stared at a series of mosaic tiles set above a pair of wooden shutters on a house in front of me. My eyes traced the roofline—I straightened up and turned on my heels, wondering at the detail of design—and a sign fixed to the oldest part of the citadel walls caught my attention.

'Almanzora Alta', the street sign read.

Our street!

'Wayne!' I shouted. 'Wayne!' I grabbed my luggage. I thrust it up a final flight of stairs. Up the hill of Al Sabikah—Wayne now following me.

Then, abandoning everything we owned, we moved across to the outer edge of the pavement—shifted from deep shadow onto a narrow outcrop of pale afternoon light—and a wide space of sky stretched before us. Behind us, nestled against the incline of the mountain, was a row of whitewashed houses, one of which, we already knew, was ours for the next twelve months. Our new home. Where we would sleep beside the borders of heaven.

Leaning over the wall that day, I was entranced by the plains rolling northwards, towards the unknown. And Wayne—Wayne entranced me—reaching for my hand with his sharp intake of breath.

'Granada is amazing, Suz. I've never seen anything like it.'

I watched him shaking his head from side to side like he couldn't believe the scene hanging in front of us. Smiling, I lifted my face into the wind and the silence. We stood side-by-side. Still.

Then, raising an arm entwined in mine, he pointed to the other side of the gorge, where a maze of cottages speckled the hillside. Packed on top of each other, with marmalade roofs and squared-off windows, the opposite neighbourhood—the Albaicin—looked like a medieval tapestry.

Green cypress trees reached between the buildings to the sky, straight as arrows, and between the dotting of houses and trees grew a clutch of cathedrals, mosques and monasteries. I could hear a thousand pigeons muttering in the arches and on the flagstones.

From the convent, down in the valley, a posy of bells started peeling. Looking back down over the rooftops, over the minarets, over the gilded domes of the mosque flashing in the sunlight, Wayne said, 'We made the right choice when we decided to come here, my love. It's going to be the best year of our lives; I promise you that.' He curled his massive arm around my waist and drew me in, stretching his coat to encompass us both.

'The past no longer matters. Till next January, everything is going to be just about you and me. The two of us, living in the moment.'

And I believed him.

Through the winter and the spring, we rested against that wall, the view tempting us out each day—clucking birds strutting around our feet. The streets, the sights, the very air was exotic and plump with possibility. Wayne was with me and I thought our happiness was infinite.

Part 1

Finding My Past

2012–2013

1

Ascot, Brisbane, July 2012

PARKED ON THE KERB OF an empty suburban street, on a Saturday afternoon, we must have looked like detectives in an old-fashioned crime novel. But with the downpour from a thunderstorm beating against the windscreen, I struggled to see what the neighbourhood even looked like.

My birth mother never made anything easy for me!

Staring at the row of two-storey structures, trying to establish a house number, I recall making a sour face at somebody's iceberg roses, fallen petals flitting across the grass. Folded in the driver's seat beside me, Wayne missed my expression because he was busy examining the security cameras dotted amongst the branches of the broad old fig trees.

So, while the windscreen wipers whined backwards and forwards, I peered through the deluge at the house opposite us—Enid's house—and fiddled with the letter in my lap, folding and refolding it, creating little shrunken shapes, fuelled by my anger.

Brisbane, January, 1992

To Miss Susan Hull,

> *The information you demanded is set out below.*

> *The man you asked about went under the name of Gerry Murphy or Gerry O'Connor or one of those other common Irish names. I can't properly remember. He claimed he was of Catholic descent and had previously worked as a police detective in Melbourne.*

Enid went on to write about her uncertainty concerning this man's appearance. About where he was born and what year. She told me he'd abandoned his pregnant wife and two children on the morning they'd left Melbourne, and how afterwards the pair had lived a nomadic existence, travelling for years from one state to another. She complained about the fact that some weeks there was enough money for food and accommodation and other weeks she went hungry while they slept in the car.

> *We broke the trip off briefly in Newcastle. We stayed in a caravan park. I had you in the hospital then we left.*

The claim she made that I found most difficult to believe was that my natural father was gambling and raising money for the IRA. To support this vocation, he apparently used a fake Irish accent and an alias.

> *Those years were the worst of my entire life. The police were chasing us. I left when they turned up on our doorstep in Perth.*

> *Contact me again, Miss Hull, and I shall seek legal advice to obtain a restraining order against you.*

> *Mrs Enid Jefferies*

I gripped the letter my birth mother had sent me, and snuck a look across at Wayne.

'I've read books about the disgrace unmarried girls felt back then—how they suffered giving up their children. Or were forced to give them up.'

He nodded, watching me.

'But my story is different. That's not how it happened when Enid gave birth to me. For twenty years I've been imagining her and my birth father in a Holden station wagon, red dust kicking up behind the tyres as they raced across the Nullarbor to Perth. The cash they'd stolen was hidden in Enid's purse, lying on the bench seat between them. She was dressed in a linen frock and her hair was whipped into a beehive.'

I paused for a minute. Flipped up the visor to try and see better. 'In a weird way, I've always fantasised my natural mother and father were Australia's answer to Bonnie and Clyde.'

Wayne grasped my fingers and the letter fluttered out of my hand.

'How much involvement do you think Enid played in all this illegal activity?' he asked.

I shrugged. 'I don't understand any of it. I never have. Obviously, he committed some kind of serious crime,' I swallowed, 'besides, of course, the fundraising for the Irish Republican Army. The IRA? Who even did that in 1961? In Australia, I mean. None of it makes sense to me. He went by this name or that . . . he was about this height . . . she thought he *may* have been born in rural Victoria somewhere. But this was the man she ran away with, the man who got her pregnant while they were being chased by the police. How could she not remember his name?'

I glanced sideways out the window again.

'Her perfect penmanship. Her personalised stationery. Those measured words.' I scowled at the rain. 'I think she's a liar.'

'Perhaps she was covering up for something else, Suz? I mean is it so vital, after all this time, to know who they were and what they were doing? Whatever happened back then, perhaps you should just leave the past where it belongs? I don't get why it's so important to you?'

I shook my head. Stared at the elegant houses surrounding us.

'It's about who I am, Wayne. I need to know about my connection to these people, and I need details.'

At last the sun ruptured the clouds and an unexpected calm arose. The rain ceased.

I twisted to face Wayne. Fright had struck me dumb. I could hardly believe what I was about to do. Clambering out of the car, a jumble of arms and legs, I raced across the tarmac, slippery from the rain, praying he would follow me. I didn't look back. I was intent. On. Just. This.

Squeezing my hand through the opening at the side of the gate, I drew back the bolt and pushed. The gate staggered open and the house loomed ahead. Pebbles skittered under my feet.

Then I was knocking.

A dog yapped from within. Solitary footsteps could be heard, treading on a wooden floor. There was a kaleidoscope of seconds. Wayne stood silent behind me; his hand spread in the curved small of my back. The door swung inwards to reveal polished timber floorboards and walls painted a rich cream. I could smell coffee.

The man at the door was reedy like a thin pipe, mild looking and myopic, with ginger hair so sparse I could see the freckled skin of his scalp beneath. He was dressed in a proper button-up shirt with cuffs, the creases in the sleeves ironed in sharply. He stood studying us over his spectacles.

'Hi . . . Hello. My name's Susan. And I think my natural mother lives here.'

Someone in the house turned up the stereo and a classical piece of music flooded the air.

'I'd better find Enid.'

Then her voice. Sounding cranky and brittle. Shouting over the melody of the music.

'Who *is* it?'

'I think you'd better come out here, dear.'

I glanced at the doormat. I remember reading and rereading the word 'welcome', trying to make sense of what I was looking at. The music inside the house shifted to a solitary violin.

I raised my head.

My mother emerged from the end of the passageway.

As the sun sidled through French doors behind her, Enid was initially in silhouette, a dark unformed shape. But her outline developed as she stepped through the light. Towards me. Narrow shoulders—like mine. She was my height, had my fine hair. Closer, and her tongue licked across dry lips: I was reminded of a blue-tongue lizard. Uneasy, the man tried to get out of her way and stumbled against the open door. It battered the wall, glancing back off him.

Enid stepped closer. I smelt the lingering odour of stale cigarettes. And as she advanced from the shadows almost, almost, I glimpsed my own face. But it was a version of me scored with wrinkles, like lines had dried in cement. It looked like my mother had smoked for a lifetime, and over the years the nicotine had coloured her face a livery yellow.

Halting at the door, hands on hips, straightening down a Jenny Kee sweater, Enid turned her head from the man clinging onto his *Sunday Mail* to us, standing on the outside pavement between her

pots of red geraniums. She was beginning to figure out that something was going on.

'You might want to talk to this lady, Enid.' The man indicated to
me with a small backward wave of his hand.

'Go turn the music off will you, Kevin?' She turned her eyes my
way. She couldn't have been less interested.

'My name is Susan Hull. I believe you're my natural mother.' I
spoke these rehearsed words clearly enough, my heart pounding in
my chest like a small girl at her first concert. Then something broke
inside me—and a fall of disconnected phrases spilled over the top of
each other: 'you left me behind', 'I was only a baby', 'why did you do
that?' The question 'who am I?' echoes in my mind now, but I don't
recall saying it at the time. It seemed most of the sensible things I'd
practised saying had dried up or clogged my throat.

The pageant fractured when Enid began 'shooing' at the two
of us, like she was shooing chooks. In her mounting hysteria, she
stumbled over one of the terracotta pots and I recollect watching
it clatter in slow motion down the driveway. I understood. In half
a second, I understood. Enid would never reveal anything about
herself or my maternal heritage: it was *her* family, *her* background.
My identity was something she saw as separate to herself, and I
didn't belong here. But I was desperate. And desperation made me
cunning. In a split second, I redirected my line of questioning.

'Well, tell me about my father then? I just want to know who he
was. What the truth is. His real name?'

The sudden change of subject seemed to feed her rising frenzy.
I could see Kevin's face over her shoulder, crumpled in worry. He
pinned a writhing terrier to his chest to stop it tearing through the
door.

'You know who the man was!' She shouted at me, her face right
up in front of mine. I could smell her sour breath.

'He was famous before he died. Everyone knew who he was. Football players were gods.' She was working frantically now with her imaginary broom—clearing us away like rubbish. It was done. Probably finished forever, my history disappearing in a witch's sweep.

'The name, the name,' I begged, shamefully aware of the sound of my pleading, unable to help myself.

'Everyone knew the name,' Enid spat through the doorway, hand tightening on the doorknob. 'Reg Taylor. From Melbourne. You *know* that.'

Then she slammed the door in my face.

I wiped the raindrops off my cheek. Reached for Wayne's hand. He shook off my hand and gently pulled me in tight for a hug. The rippling sound of magpies filled my ears.

Reg Taylor. Who the hell was Reg Taylor? I stared over Wayne's shoulder at the grey Brisbane skyline. Despite what Enid had said, I'd never heard of the man. After years of struggling to accept one version of the truth, I now had two different explanations about who I was.

2

Dubbo, September 2012

AFTER THE MEETING WITH ENID, Wayne and I gave up on our holiday in Queensland and returned home to the central west: to country New South Wales. Back then, Wayne leased a garden flat in Orange for the nights he was working shifts at the mine, and his weeks off were spent with me in my cottage. Built in 1885, it was situated down a dirt track, five kilometres outside Dubbo. From our front veranda there were no other houses in sight, just endless reaches of green lucerne paddock and cattle, and far away, the view of a slow-moving stretch of the Macquarie River.

The original timber-panelled rooms of the house were small, perfectly square and low—with logs a hundred years old still propping up the old tin roof. For two adults the size was barely satisfactory: two bedrooms led directly off the living room (one we used as an office), there was a remodelled kitchen, the lounge room—painted lemon to catch the light through the low windows—and a renovated bathroom. The original wide wooden floorboards creaked. The brick fireplace was half the length of the external wall and the cottage was set on almost an acre of its own land. I adored the house.

Wayne, at 185 centimetres tall, found it frustratingly tiny, I think, but he never complained.

We'd met online, in early 2012, before all the driving and criss-crossing around Australia to track down Enid and my birth father. On a dating website for 'mature-aged' Australians, he'd listed Sebastian Faulks as his favourite writer and so had I. Penning long emails to each other, we discussed philosophy, favourite books, political opinions—and a dream to leave Australia behind for a year and live somewhere exotic before we grew too old. We fell half in love before we'd even met.

> Why I love to read? Because of the notion that I'm out of step with others around me. What is written in books seems more accessible to me than what I've experienced in the real world. I was a fat child, I wore glasses, I was adopted. Didn't belong anywhere. Books were always a better place for me . . .

His reply:

> Often, it's loneliness that moves one to books. That's what it often was when I was a boy, and later a young man—when I found myself removed from the mainstream. Isolated from others. Then books kept me company. I am the only person I know who has read *Poor Fellow My Country*.

From that first email, it only took a month and a half before we met in person. I was standing inside at home, watching him— framed through the living room window—as he unlatched the front gate. He looked more serious than I'd expected, and taller: well over six feet. A bear of a man dressed in Levi's and a dark blue cotton shirt with the sleeves rolled up to the elbows. He had the most beautiful, broad, brown forearms I'd ever seen, and his shoulders were hard and wide. His chin was squared off like an old Hollywood movie star. Wayne looked like a man who knew the way the world ran. A man who knew what was what.

'I'm three years out of a long-term relationship,' was one of the first things he said to me—after he settled on the lounge and I served us coffee. Running his hand across the top of his cropped head of hair, he seemed very honest and straightforward.

'I've been married three times,' I said with a blush, not quite meeting his eyes. But it didn't faze him.

He shrugged. 'Which story about the past ever tells us the exact truth about a person?'

Then, somewhere around our fifth date: 'We've no time to muck about, Suz. Both of us have had a lifetime of bad relationships.'

He was the first one to say he was in love. And how could I fail to fall for a man who understood the significance of language, yet asked me to judge him by his actions? Words are important, he would say to me, but the actions of a man demonstrate his true intent. So, I loved him to begin with because I was amazed any man could recognise such a distinction, let alone ask me to measure his character by it. All the men I'd known said one thing and meant another. The notion of 'character' was never discussed. I thought his request demonstrated his self-confidence and self-awareness. It showed me he was genuine.

As the months went by, I felt I'd discovered a man who was the person he said he was. His words were backed up with an easy steadfastness. Plans were stuck to. We swapped books. Talked about a year in Spain.

He said, 'I love to travel, to wander down a street I've never been in before. I could spend the rest of my life visiting a new city every night.' His dreams were echoes of my own.

But in other ways, he brought new strength into my life. One morning, early in our relationship, I received a letter from my solicitor informing me that my ex-partner Joe was demanding a 60/40 split in our divorce settlement. I could see Wayne through the French doors, in the fine mist of the garden, flannelette shirtsleeves pushed up, chopping wood for me under the old gum tree. A curl of love for him spooled through me. Gratitude, trust and respect. I watched as the muscles moved in his shoulders underneath his shirt. His face was stern in concentration; his legs, clothed in denim, stood wide apart.

Wandering outside, I squatted on one of the bigger pieces of wood. I explained to him that I was tempted to give in to my ex because, 'I would rather get something than nothing'.

Wayne struck the axe blade into the ironbark with one powerful action, and turned to me.

'Suz, it should be fifty-fifty. You worked hard. You earnt more money than him. Don't give in to him. Hold onto your dignity and remember, I've got your back.'

'But what if Joe just keeps going? What if all the money is swallowed up in solicitors' fees. What if I end up with less?'

'Hold your ground, Suz. Stay calm. Don't allow fear to get in your way. You have to stand up for yourself.'

So, back home, after learning about Reg Taylor, I knew enough about my man to spend the next few days trying not to make a fuss. He didn't like fuss and bother. He didn't like too much emotion. Quietly I made my phone calls, unobtrusively trawling the internet for information, discovering all I could about my birth father's heritage and his famous football career. But randomly, throughout the week, I'd make excuses to seek out a mirror, to stare at myself, searching my face for long minutes, trying to identify features I may have overlooked for the past half a century. For all the wrong reasons the song *Turning Japanese* played over and over in my head. Because yes, oh yes—not only did it turn out Reg Taylor had actually existed—he'd been a well-known, well-liked VFL player from Melbourne—he was also one quarter Chinese and 100 per cent dead.

'Okay, let's get this straight,' Wayne said to me on the following Saturday afternoon. He was preparing to return to work, for a seven-day shift in the mine. Underground work. Explosives. Responsibility for a large team of men. Things I knew little about. Standing in front of the cupboard, he folded his work shirts methodically, laid them flat in the suitcase lying open on the bed. He paused and looked at me.

'Because Enid was born in Smith Creek and grew up there, and we found out Taylor played football there in 1959, you think that's when she slept with him? That's when you were conceived?'

I was sprawled across our large wooden-framed bed, with Millie my dog curled up snugly next to my shoulder. 'Yep.'

Wayne dragged his high-visibility trousers off the shelf. Moved from the cupboard to the case and back again, talking all the way.

'Then you think, because she was ashamed of her story being so stereotypical, or ashamed of the circumstances, your mother devised a story about your father being an IRA fundraiser, to cover up the banality of the truth?'

Even to me, even then, it sounded a little odd.

'I don't know why she made up that story about the Irishman. But I think that Reg Taylor seems a more logical candidate for my birth father. The only thing I can think to do is to go down to Smith Creek. Try and find out more. It's the only lead I have.'

But there were other things that didn't add up. Why, for instance, had Enid insisted I already knew my birth father's name? Why was my date of birth listed two years after Taylor had left Smith Creek behind?

Wayne zipped the suitcase shut, turned to face me.

'Okay. We'll take a trip down to Smith Creek. See what we can find out; see if there are people who still remember the two of them. But the whole bloody thing sounds so ludicrous!'

I knelt up and hugged him, kissing his face with a loud smacking sound. Millie whined in her sleep.

But Wayne wasn't finished. He stepped back and held me at arm's length.

'Just promise me this search won't carry you too far away from me. What's happened in the past can't define who you are, you know that. The past mustn't dictate the present.'

Nodding, I laid my cheek against the much-washed cloth of his shirt, listened to what he was telling me, and wondered: did this appeal come from something that had made his past difficult? Relationships turned wrong in years gone by? He was always so insistent about us needing to live in the present. Whereas for me, moving into a future with him—something I desperately wanted— could only be achieved if I understood every aspect of what had gone before. I wanted a life with Wayne. I loved Wayne. But I also needed to understand the truth about who I was. And because I was crazy about him, I now appreciate that I failed to recognise just how significant this disparity between the two of us was.

At Smith Creek, we'd booked into one of those generic country motels, with a neon sign advertising rooms for ninety-four dollars a night. The hotel owner, missing some bottom teeth, talked slowly but responded with that open-handedness that so many country people possess.

She handed over the keys to our room, scribbled down the breakfast order, told us the best place in town for steak was the RSL. Unfortunately, she had no relevant information about Reg Taylor.

'Anyone else you can suggest? Who I can ask about Reg I mean, or Enid Nilsdoter?' Nilsdoter, I explained, was my mother's maiden name.

She promised to ring someone she knew while we took our bags upstairs to the room.

'By the time you come down I'll have an answer for you.'

Wayne swung the ute through the broad streets, past a shuttered corner shop padlocked for the night and an arid-looking football field. I heard a shift in the gears as we drew up outside a brick house, set behind a concrete wall.

Pushing the hair off my face and without moving my eyes from the building I muttered, 'It doesn't look like it's changed in forty years.'

'Well, you don't need to go in,' Wayne said. 'Leave it for another day, if you want? We can always grab a pizza, have an early night at the motel. Get an early start tomorrow.'

But I couldn't turn away.

Wayne had different ideas. He twisted around in his seat and I could feel him staring at me.

'Look at me, Suz.'

I sighed. Turned away from the house and concentrated over his shoulder, out through the window on *his* side of the car. A neighbour across the road was unpacking his work tools from a white ute and I saw, more than heard, the metal clunk as he lugged the tool bag off the back of the tray.

'I don't want to lecture. But this whole ... obsession.' He raised his hands in exasperation, and as I began to protest, he growled, 'Let me finish.'

'You're too taken up by it all.' He turned my chin with his finger, till I was looking him in the eye. It was the closest we'd ever come to having an argument.

'I agreed to come down here with you. But it's late tonight. Too late.' He shook his head. 'Someone, whoever ... made a mistake in the past. Whether it was your mother or your father, who knows ... everyone has secrets.' He swallowed. 'But you shouldn't be focusing on that. You should be focusing on us, and the future. I want us both to live for now.'

'You've got to understand.' I clutched his hand. 'This search is about discovering who I am. If I don't know the truth about what happened back then, how can I have an authentic connection with you? And live my life the way I should? Whatever Enid is hiding, that's my history too. It belongs to me. The past just can't be denied. And I'm so tired of everyone else knowing about it, and no one telling me. It makes me really ...' and I hissed, '*really* angry.'

'Liz dying ... and my mum so sick. It's made me realise life is short. I have a right to the truth and I need to know now. Before *everyone* dies!' Even I could hear the panic in my voice.

'Suz, most people lie out of self-preservation.' He paused. It was his turn to gaze out the window. 'They lie because they don't want to hurt the person they love ... or maybe because they're scared that person will see them differently if they know what the truth really is.' There was a note in his voice that day that made me pause for a moment. But I was too wound up to pay it much attention.

3

Smith Creek, September 2012

RAPPING ON LILL THOMPSON'S DOOR that night, I knew Wayne was right. It was too late to be arriving unannounced. She was, after all, a ninety-year-old woman living on her own. But I had an irrational fear that she would die during the night and I would never find out whether she had any knowledge to share. Apparently, she had been close to the Nilsdoter family.

'Who is it?' the old lady bawled through the door.

'My name is Susan Hull,' I shouted. 'I'm the daughter Enid Nilsdoter gave up for adoption. I was told you might have information about my family?'

The door cracked open, and Lill Thompson peered through the space.

'Do you have any ID, love?'

I fumbled through my bag, flipped it open to my driver's licence and pushed it up flat to the split between the door and the frame.

'Hang on. Just let me get my specs.'

I sighed. Five long minutes dragged by till the stretch of light was backfilled by her shape.

Lill peered at my wallet again. 'Thanks, love.' Then she unlocked the bolt and shuffled aside to let me in.

But she was sharp. With her glasses halfway down her nose she'd picked out Wayne still sitting in the car.

'He your husband?'

Nodding, because even though we weren't married at that stage, it was easier just to go along with her. 'Yes.'

'He better come in, too,' the old woman muttered.

We waited in silence on the floral, overstuffed couch while Lill made the tea. She came back from the kitchen, set down an old, cracked porcelain plate stacked high with gingerbread biscuits and served us tea.

'Actually, I've been waiting for this day for a while, love. I've got a real lot to say to you!'

I squeezed my fingers together, tried to resist the urge to pick at my nails. I remember wondering vaguely how she'd known I'd turn up.

'You are Enid's daughter. No doubt about it in my mind. You're the spitting image of her. Bit skinnier than Enid, but I'd have known you, even if you hadn't told me.' With quaking fingers, she stretched forward and touched my cheek. I shifted uncomfortably. She turned her attention to the biscuits and clawed at the pile before collapsing back into her chair.

'You look a bit like Daphne, too.'

'Daphne?'

'Enid's mother. *Your* grandmother. My best friend.' Her face closed into sad folds. 'We were friends for more than sixty years, Daph and me.' Lill munched absently on the biscuit. Roused herself.

'I suppose you wanna know more about your mother? Who your father was?'

'Yes, please, Mrs Thompson.' I sat straight and proper, like a schoolgirl.

'Well. As I always used to say to Daph, she was an "odd bod", that Enid of hers. And a bit too high and mighty. Too proud for her own good. They say it comes before a fall.' Lill sniffed unattractively.

'I 'member, Bob, my dear departed, would go 'round Saturdays to do their lawn. Enid would lie under a big old gum tree growing in the back yard, reading a book, cool as a cucumber. Never raised a smile. Never offered to help. She always had 'er nose poked in a book.'

According to Lill, Enid was also jealous of her sister who looked just like a movie star. She, apparently, was everything 'poor old Enid' wasn't.

'I 'member we had them two kids sat in the bath once and I said to Daph, "Enid is a plain Jane, that's all there is to it, and you can't do nothing about it." Daph shushed me though everyone was saying it. Margaret, on the other hand, was beautiful.

'She ended up marrying a rich businessman from Melbourne, a few years before he died. Inherited all his money. I knew she would. What Margaret wanted she always got.'

Judging now was the time to interrupt, '. . . and Enid? She didn't have a boyfriend?'

Lill snatched up another biscuit. In between bites, '. . . not till Reg whathisname came along.' She indicated at me with crumbs sticking to her fingers, 'Your father.'

I inched forward.

'Good-looking he was. But bad news for Enid. He was married already, see? But she fell for him heavy. Like a pig in muck. Even when he told her to leave him alone, she couldn't give him up. Always waiting outside the door of the changing shed for him.

'One night it got real bad. Frank, your grandfather, was called down to the club. Enid had taken an overdose of something.' Lill began to whisper. 'Frank sent her to Melbourne for a while, to a special place. Of course, we all knew by then she was pregnant. With you.' Her eyes focused on me.

'But you don't look Chinese at all, love, if you don't mind me sayin'? Reg was Chinese you know?'

My smile, I knew by then, must have appeared very feeble.

'He was a good man, though, despite all that. Even after getting Enid up the duff. He and his wife offered to take the baby; I mean you ...' She ended in confusion.

'Your grandma and your aunt, Margaret, wanted to keep you, too. But Enid would have nothing of it ... She stayed in Melbourne afterwards, and I've never seen her since. Hadn't really so much as thought about her till I got your letter.'

I tilted my head.

'My letter?'

Lill didn't hear me, she was so intent on spilling everything she knew. She carried on as if I'd never spoken.

'But I was thinking there, dear, about who else you could be asking about all this. There was a neighbour. Lionel Rigby. He did good. He wrote a book about growing up in Smith Creek. He knew the girls real well. He wrote about Enid and Margaret in that book of his. You could talk to him. Or read his book?'

'Mrs Thompson,' I repeated, talking over the top of her, 'what letter?'

'The one you sent me from Melbourne, dear. Must have been, what, two years ago?'

'What?'

'Two years ago. A letter from you. From Melbourne. You aren't from Melbourne?'

25

I recall Wayne heaving himself up closer beside me. I recall him resting his hand over the top of mine. 'No,' Wayne said, speaking slowly. 'We're not even from Victoria, Mrs Thompson.'

'Look, I have here . . .' I ferreted in my bag for my original birth certificate. Flourished the document at Lill Thompson.

'Here, you can see. I was born in Newcastle, NSW, May, 1961. Mother named as Enid Nilsdoter from Smith Creek. Baby unnamed.'

'Well, I'll be. I didn't think I was getting that old.' She glanced up. 'Hang on a sec, luv, while I go and find that letter. It's in me dressin' table bureau.'

As she limped from the room, I turned and faced Wayne. 'What on earth is going on here? This is so strange.'

Within minutes, one hand palming along pieces of furniture to keep her balance, Lill hobbled back in. She had a hand-written letter raised in her other fist in triumph.

'Here it is, girl. From Susan Dewy. Isn't that you? Says you were born in 1959 to Enid Nilsdoter.'

The pounding silence of the night seemed to roar in my ears.

Eventually, I reached for the letter, verified the contents: a name, and a Victorian address; the attached photocopy of a birth certificate so similar to mine, only the place of birth and the date were different. But this little baby was not me. Because this little baby had been named at birth.

Wayne spoke. 'Same mother. And she was named Susan. But it's not you, Suz.'

Turning to him with my eyes wide open, I tried to negotiate my thoughts through the shock.

'There are two of us? With exactly the same name? And she got rid of both of us?'

4

Dubbo, September 2012

WE WERE IN THE KITCHEN, unpacking the dishwasher, and I was in a mood to be reasonable—almost. I think the twelve-hour drive home the day before had partially numbed me to reality.

'My theory goes like this,' I passed Wayne a wine glass. He duly held it to the light to check it was clean. 'Back then, Enid was the only one who knew she'd given up *two* baby daughters. The other people in her family knew she'd fallen pregnant in Smith Creek, that she'd delivered a baby in Melbourne and that she'd called the baby Susan.

'But who knew about me? The baby born eighteen months later while my mother was on the run?

'So, if I'm such a secret, perhaps Enid only told Kevin the Melbourne story? But she kept my birth hush-hush, from him, and from everyone else, because how would it look?'

'Makes sense, Suz.'

I clicked the dishwasher door shut and turned to him. 'In Brisbane, Enid was panicking, desperately hoping we'd get off the doorstep before you and I, and possibly Kevin, realised we were discussing a separate adoption—mine. A different little girl. That's why she spoke about Reg. That's why she insisted I already knew about him.'

But the next day, after Wayne had returned to work, all my rational thinking fell to pieces. Emotion barrelled in. And I collapsed on the bed and thought back to the beginning of my journey to find my birth parents. How I'd first begun the search. It had been over twenty years ago.

Back in 1991, I'd tracked down Enid's sister, Margaret, who was unmarried at that time. I explained to her, during a phone call, how the government had made it legal for adopted children to access their original birth certificates. That I'd applied for mine as soon as I could. How I'd made the link between my mother's surname on the certificate and hers.

'Well, even though we're sisters and we were once very close,' she had said, 'I'm afraid Enid no longer speaks to me. I have to warn you, dear; she will be furious if you try and contact her. But here's the phone number, if you really want it . . .'

The phone number for my natural mother.

How easy I thought it was going to be that day.

But after the initial shock, after Enid understood who I was, she proved Margaret's words true. She asked me if I was after money.

'Because don't expect it.'

I explained anxiously, 'It's not money I'm after. I just want information about myself. And I want to share information with you. I have a son,' I pronounced. 'Your grandchild.' But she wasn't interested.

'I have absolutely no curiosity about your life. Or your current situation. I've tried very hard, for many years, to forget what happened in Newcastle.'

I protested, but my voice weakened with every word.

'Can you please just give me the information I want, Mrs Jefferies? I promise not to bother you again. Who was my father? What about medical histories? What about . . .'

But her voice rose hysterically.

'I warn you; I'm going to hang up on you. How *dare* you call me now! You are *never, ever* to contact me again. Don't talk to me about what we have in common. We have nothing in common.'

I crumpled into the chair, sobbing. My adoptive mum, Carol, gently took the phone from me. I remember her repeating, *Susan is a good girl. She is a good girl. She just wants to know about her past.*

I wrote to Enid soon after that phone call. My shame and sadness had shifted to fury. I argued about my ethical rights. About my right to know my background. Hence the letter—those two pages she deigned to send back—information that was next to useless. Then there was no communication between us until 2012, two decades later, when Wayne and I drove to Brisbane.

As I unpacked the suitcase from our drive to Smith Creek, did the laundry, collected Millie from the boarding kennels, I moved in a trance. Because dancing round and round in my head was one dominant idea: *she had two of us.* To me, the words were like the sound of water rushing over stones; everything else receding into the background. Who knew what this other Susan might be able to tell me?

I shoved the washing basket back in the laundry and I dialled my sister's number.

The call rang out!

I dialled again and again. But there was no response.

During another desperate attempt the following evening, the

recorded voice asked for the caller to 'please leave a message, as the residents of the house are otherwise occupied'.

The following morning, I hastily gulped down a too-hot cup of coffee. Burnt the tip of my tongue. Punched in the numbers, announcing to myself with emphasis on each press of my index finger: 'This. Is. For. You. Enid. Because. YOU. Wouldn't. Tell. Me!'

'Helloooooa?'

'Hi. I was wondering if I could speak with Susan Dewy?'

'Speaking.'

Catching a breath, I commenced.

5

Melbourne, October 2012

MY HANDS WERE TANGLED IN my lap. Looking at my half-sister's face, it seemed she was as terrified as me. But the likeness between us was indisputable. Even the waitress mumbled something about how nice it was for sisters to have the chance to share a coffee together.

Both of us had the same full lower lip. Her eyebrows were as fine as mine. And I knew why she wore that trouser suit—because under it, her ankles would be thick and solid, just like mine.

The first thing she said was, 'It's like looking into a mirror.' Her voice emerged with a bit of a squeak. Then she stretched her arm across the red-and-white checked tablecloth and clasped my fingers in hers.

Around us, I could hear the chatter of other patrons, the hiss of the cappuccino machine, crockery being slammed onto hard surfaces. All the clamorous sounds of a morning rush hour. But at our table, we were separate from the chaos. We were silent, gazing at each other's faces.

Her bearing was stiff and her movements were considered. She was dressed very conservatively—I thought it made her look older than she was. Her trouser suit had been bought from somewhere like David Jones or Myer.

I was wearing my customary black jeans and a pullover, and I'd added a green silk scarf—the one my best friend, Di, had picked up for me as a birthday present a few years ago. It was looped around my neck for good luck. One foot, in its flat leather shoe, rested awkwardly atop the other.

There were so many questions I wanted to ask her, but I began with the obvious.

'It's so strange we have the same name. Don't you think?'

'Enid named me,' the other Susan said. Then she ducked her head, searched for something deep within the stiff bag on her lap. The bag gleamed in its patent leather blackness. She squeezed it to her like a talisman before laying a manila folder between us.

'The social worker compiled this information about my adoption. She handed it to my adoptive parents. It's all in here.' My sister tapped it with a carefully filed nail. 'I was told I'm lucky to have it. It's unusual to have such access apparently. The documents state that Enid called me Susan immediately after I was born.'

She paused. 'How did you get your name?'

'When the doctor gave me to my adoptive parents, they named me Susan. Mine was what was called a private adoption. The doctor had put the word out that there was a baby and Newcastle was a small place. Mum and Dad turned up at the doctor's practice with a reference from Dad's boss and the GP simply handed me over.'

'Very different circumstances to me,' said Susan. 'Everything in that folder methodically records the conditions under which I was relinquished.' And she lowered her face.

'Can you tell me?'

'It's simple, really. Enid got pregnant in her home town to a married man. She came to Melbourne to give birth to me.' Then Susan pushed the folder across the laminated table.

'Read it,' she encouraged, fingers back clenching at the handbag in her lap.

26.8.58
Enid came in this morning with her mother. Mother said she and her husband will get a flat for the two sisters and she thinks Enid will be well occupied looking after the flat and Margaret. Both Enid and mother asked about adoption procedures, which were explained to them. Enid left the room and mother told me her daughter has held down several quite good jobs but is inclined to flare up and leave if she becomes displeased.

2.12.58.
I had a longish talk with Enid this morning. She seems an intelligent lass. Said she loves to read. She has decided on the adoption of the coming infant.

2.2.59
Enid had baby girl.

6.2.59.
Enid is still wanting the babe to be adopted, appeared to be quite calm. Has called the child 'Susan'. Her mother has been down with a close friend, Mrs Lillian Thompson, who was offering support. Mother said she and her husband are desperate to take the baby but Enid forbids it and is determined to sign the adoption papers.

Resting my chin in my palm I glanced up, meeting my sister's gaze. The truth about her entry into the world was in some ways worse than mine and the sympathy I felt for her was extraordinary. It threw me off balance. Somehow, I had thought we were equal. Or the same. Or something. The world tilted beneath my feet a little. Our connection was less than I'd imagined.

'I honestly don't know what to say, Susan.'

A dishevelled young woman, tray in hand, interrupted us briefly. 'Would you like anything else, ladies?'

'More coffee? Some cake?' I asked my sister, who gave a small nod.

While we waited, I thought about the question I most wanted to ask, decided just to blurt it out.

'Have you ever met Enid?'

Susan shook her head. 'I wrote to the authorities asking for a lift on the veto. But the decision was binding. Even though I had access to the information about my adoption, I didn't have her approval to meet in person.'

Our coffee arrived. And she fiddled with her mug, twisting it backwards and forwards in never-completed circles.

'Also, I've always been worried about how my parents would feel if I went searching. I didn't want to make them feel like they weren't loved. That I wasn't grateful for what they'd done for me.'

'I completely understand. About not wanting to hurt people, I mean—and the veto thing too. Liz, my best friend . . .' I paused. Attempted to make what I was saying sound coherent.

'I had two best friends at school. Liz and Di. They were—are— like sisters to me. But Liz passed away from cancer last year. It was devastating because she was so young and the cancer was unex- pected. Her daughters are distressed. Confused. Her husband is lost.' I took a deep breath. 'Then a month after Liz died, my brother and I had to make the decision to move our adoptive mother, Carol, into a nursing home. She was diagnosed with Alzheimer's disease five years ago.'

Susan kept her head down.

'It was immediately afterwards, after her diagnosis, during the terrible whirl of appointments with specialists, the pleading and arguing about the need for my mum to relinquish her driver's licence, all the sneaky telephone calls I made arranging home care, that I started thinking again about this "other" mother.'

I leant forward. If anyone could understand, this woman could.

'Carol was the mother who pored over the Butterick pattern book and measured and stitched all my childhood clothes. It was Carol who baked me chocolate cakes, who cried at my university graduation. Now she lives in a nursing home—and she no longer knows who I am. Meanwhile, all this time, I've had this other mother, this parallel woman, in a parallel universe, whom I'd never met.'

Susan finally moved. She raised her eyes to my face. She understood.

'Liz . . . my friend who I said died last year?'

Susan nodded.

'Liz was adopted too—and like you, she had a veto placed on the facts relating to her adoption.' I shifted in my seat, bit my lip till I tasted blood. 'No meetings were allowed between Liz and her mother. No father was named. But significantly, she was denied access to any medical knowledge. Medical knowledge that might have helped. Because she died from cancer at forty-nine.'

'I'm very sorry for your loss,' my sister said.

I smiled, felt fresh pain contract my heart. Stepped with delicacy through what I had to say next.

'What about your father?'

Susan shrugged her shoulders, her eyes fixed on her lap. 'He wasn't named in the papers. You saw it. You read it. The whole procedure was documented very carefully.'

We both found other places to look. I felt discouraged. I'd been hoping for so much more than this. I'd been hoping for an alliance. Answers. Identity.

'Well, I've met Enid.'

'She isn't a very nice person, is she?'

I shook my head.

'I've thought so much about my own past,' Susan continued. 'Now I know my mother's family were more than willing to take care of me but that Enid wouldn't allow it. Well . . . that makes me realise how deeply unhappy she must have been.'

I remember then considering my dilemma: to tell Susan about her father or not? Seriously, there wasn't a choice, was there? I would want to know if it were me. Yet I wasn't sure—I was beginning to learn that not everyone believed the past was important. Not in the same way I did.

'Susan, I know who your father is.' But there was no quickening of her blue eyes as anticipated. No straightening up or leaning forward.

'Do you want me to tell you?' I asked her.

'It really doesn't matter anymore,' she said. 'I was adopted because my adoptive parents were unable to bear a child. They were kind and they were devoted to me.

'I thought, when I was a child, that it was vital I find Enid. That's why I made enquiries when I got older. Now? I'm not so certain. A doctor once told me that the thing adopted people most fear is that they will be abandoned a second time. I don't want to risk that.'

'Okay. That's okay. I understand.'

When I rang Susan four weeks later, her husband answered. Brusquely he informed me they would prefer it if all communication between us ceased. It was better she concentrated on the reality of the present. The less said about what happened in the past, the better.

'You understand, Susan?'

Was that an aside? Was he talking to her or to me? I'm still not sure, even now.

6

Newcastle, November 2012

IN SPITE OF ALL THE travelling Wayne and I undertook in 2012, and the challenges we experienced trying to make sense of the myriad details surrounding my birth, each month I needed to make the ten-hour round trip from Dubbo back to Newcastle, for a weekend visit with my mum. She couldn't speak anymore. She couldn't move, other than to compulsively stick her fingers in her mouth and pull them out again. She didn't understand who I was, or comprehend what I said to her. Sometimes, my brother, Pete, and I visited the nursing home together. Or when Di was up from Sydney visiting her parents, she would sit with me. And I could concentrate on something other than tugging the damp, oversized bib my mother wore back down over her chest, to stop her trying to swallow her own fists.

My best friend and I had known each other since we were children. With Liz, we had been an airtight group of three. We were like a set of Tupperware boxes with the lids fixed on so firmly you could not prise them off. Not even using your fingertips.

At eleven, we'd labelled ourselves *LSD,* using the initials of our first names. We enlarged upon the idea with a personal tag line:

LSD against the world 4 eva. From then on, everything we owned, from our books to our pencil cases, even our school cases, was emblazoned with that proclamation.

At thirteen, we bought matching coloured t-shirts and ironed the letters *LSD* on the front; we wore the t-shirts everywhere, keen to promote our identity: to demonstrate that we belonged to each other and that we were different to everyone else. But in reality, of course, we were just innocent little girls, growing up in the 1970s, indulging in the mildest of teenage rebellion: smoking in Liz's bathroom, wagging school in favour of a visit to the cinema where, slunk low in the seats, we watched adult-rated movies like *Equus.* My claim to fame was acting on impulse—like flagging a car down on the road that ran beside the oval after our masochistic P.E. teacher made us run laps. 'Asthma attack,' I huffed when dropped at the school office. Di and I would also often bunk off the maths tutoring our parents had arranged for us, and buy two dollars' worth of cabanossi from the pizza shop to eat in the park. Sitting on the grass, we thought ourselves to be very outré. Di was always up for an ill-advised walk along the cliffs when high tide was coming up, and was willing to sit beside me in Hunter Street while I read palms to make extra pocket money, because I couldn't sing, so busking wasn't an option.

But our friendship was especially important for Liz, because her adoptive father had died when she was eleven and, soon after, her adoptive mother suffered a nervous breakdown. Liz spent more time at my house or Di's than at her own. She was the wariest of the three of us. The most careful.

The year we turned sixteen, we spent the summer holidays together at a place on the coast. From sunrise to sunset the three of us wandered by the ocean, wearing feathers in our ears, bikinis— even me, a recent convert to Weight Watchers—and Hawaiian shirts tied in a knot above our bellies. We raced barefoot across the sand, rolled in the surf, snacked on salt and vinegar chips. Boz Scaggs played on the transistor radio. It was a perfect time. Possibly the most perfect time in my life.

What was special about our friendship was the way we remained genuine friends all the way into adulthood: sharing flats together, sharing marriage celebrations, the births of our children, our various careers, our divorces.

Then Liz died.

I was in New York, visiting the city for the first time, when Caitlin called. I jumped on the first flight home. Wrote the eulogy on the plane. Caught a connecting flight to Canberra. Geoff, Liz's husband, and the girls, Caitlin and Ashleigh, met me at the airport. We hugged, everyone suffering from shock.

When Di and I saw each other, we literally fell into the other's arms. We could not stop crying.

We were not invincible. Part of who we were had vanished. Gone where, I kept asking Di. She can't just be *gone*!

At the funeral, there were so many people: they were lining the footpaths outside the church. To mourn the loss of our beautiful friend.

Later, at the wake, I was reminded of something that had happened fifteen years ago—when Mum had still been well and my son Jonno was only a boy.

We'd travelled to Newcastle for the weekend. I'd woken up late on Saturday morning. I could hear Jonno next door, laughing, playing with the neighbour's dog. Wandering into the kitchen, I glanced out onto the back balcony. Mum was sitting in her favourite chair, sobbing. I'd never seen her cry before. Not even when Dad had died.

'Mum, what on earth's wrong?'

'Robin passed away last night,' she said, and she kept weeping into her handkerchief.

Later, after I made her a cup of tea, she said to me, 'When your best friend dies, a part of you dies, too. Because you and she are the only ones who share the same memories. Without your best friend to laugh or cry over those recollections, your childhood dies. No one else is left who remembers what you remember.'

So, in Canberra, Di and I made a pact—we would never take our friendship for granted—it was to remain insoluble no matter what happened. Because the kind of grief we were suffering was something only the two of us could comprehend. We were the only ones who could appreciate what LSD had meant. And that shared experience made us tighter than ever. We became gatekeepers for each other's past—the one we had shared with Liz.

Liz's death also made me very aware of the passage of time, and heightened the real possibility of death. All of a sudden, I was in a hurry to do everything. The frightening idea that I might run out of time made me panic. Everything had to be done *now*. Because if Liz had disappeared, so could I.

The year that she died, I left my difficult relationship with Joe. And Di and I travelled to Borneo and trekked through the jungle. I'd been declared close to legally blind two weeks before the trip, due to cataracts, and Dianne had broken her wrist—these factors deterred neither of us. Desperation about Liz's death pushed us beyond the realms of rationality for a while.

But Borneo was restorative. We ate too much at high tea in the polished marble halls of our hotel, and put ourselves in silly situations, the way only middle-aged women seem to do. We clung together when, on a broken boardwalk in the jungles of Sabah, Di saw our first wild orangutan through the canopy of green foliage.

He hurtled through the grass at us, the wood thumping under our feet when he climbed onto the boardwalk. Standing motionless, gripping each other's hands, we stared in absolute silence as the animal swung himself onto the railing, only feet away. As we contemplated him with solemn intent—just as he regarded us—the beauty of the world overwhelmed us.

Back in Dubbo, I moved into the little house on the outskirts of the city, vowing to make a new life for myself. Even though it had been nearly twenty years, I started thinking about Enid again. Because it felt like time was running out. My mum was dying. And two out of the three women whom I depended upon most in the world had now disappeared.

'She seems pretty much the same,' Di said to me, 'since last time I saw her.'

I glanced at my best friend's face, squinting against the light to see her better, to appreciate all that she meant to me. As she'd so often said, we'd been through enough together to be able to say anything to each other.

'Yep.' I bent the straw I'd stuck into the plastic cup and inserted it between Mum's lips. Warm tea was her favourite.

I stretched my legs out. Poked my Doc Martens into a square of sun on the lawn. We'd wheeled Mum into the courtyard to enjoy the early summer weather. What good I thought vitamin D would do escapes me, but it was more pleasant than sitting in the communal lounge room.

'So, tell me about your sister. I can't imagine what that must have been like for you.'

'God, where do I start?'

My best friend leant over my mum and hugged me; arms folded about my neck. I watched the leaves over her shoulder skip around in little whirly whirlys under the gum tree. There was a summer storm coming. Mum lay impassively beneath the weight of our embrace. Little baby noises and bubbles escaped from her mouth.

Sitting back in the chair, I started to explain the inexplicable.

'I always tried to escape the sense of uncertainty adoption instilled in me. Always attached myself to men too quickly. Always believed I wasn't good enough. But my sister ... I don't know. I think she's reacted in the opposite way. She holds herself back from life ...' I shrugged.

'Throughout my childhood, people seemed to think it was okay to comment on my plainness and my eccentricities. You know what it was like ... I was loved, but I wasn't the same as Mum and Dad. Or Pete ... I remember Mum dragging me to bridal tea showers, sewing circles ... trying to play sport. Watching sport. It was all so important to everyone else—but I preferred my books.'

'But you always made your own way, hun. Be proud of that. And things are different for you now. You've got Wayne. You belong with him one hundred per cent. He's the only man I've ever seen you with who really gets you. We've been friends for how long? Since fifth class, right? How many boyfriends, lovers and husbands of yours have I met?'

I laughed. Sipped my coffee.

'He understands you. He appreciates you. He cares so much about you. I wish any man had ever cared that much about me. It gives the rest of us hope that romance isn't quite dead yet!'

And she laughed too, and we hugged again in the garden on that stormy summer afternoon. Mum's little face creased in half too. She had no idea what we were laughing about but she mimicked our smiles hopefully.

7

Dubbo, November 2012

That Sunday night, after driving hundreds of kilometres home, Wayne was waiting for me in the low doorway. He'd finished work that morning. Greeted me with a massive bear hug, his face split in a large grin. We made love by the firelight.

Then we cooked together. And for me, it was these unhurried manoeuvres around the kitchen, replete after the ampleness of sex, that made me feel tangible.

'How was your mum, love?'

'The same.'

'And Di?'

'She's talking about moving back to Newcastle!'

I was concentrating on scooping up the diced tomatoes, arranging the vegetables in a baking dish. He was busy pulling onions off the shelf, examining each one for any flaws.

'I was giving some thought, Suz, when I was at work. To what happens next.' He discarded one onion and picked up another.

'First, I was thinking about that neighbour bloke. Rigby? You know . . . that fella Lill told you about?

'That book you've been reading of his has explained a lot about Enid—about her pride and her determination even if those charac-teristics are, or were, misplaced.' And he smiled. 'I can see similarities between you and your mother.'

I'd spent the previous week staying up late every night, reading *Rigby Rules*.

. . . Enid was back from Dublin. We smoke, drank strong coffee, and while I lazed in her flat, we listened to the Rolling Stones and she read me passages from the letters of James Joyce.

Rigby then listed all of the books on Enid's shelves, some of which were on my bookshelves, and described how the two of them spent whole weekends discussing Whitlam and Nixon and kibbutz in Israel.

Enid was strong-minded, intellectual, challenging. She didn't let one make a point without dissecting it to pieces. She encouraged me to travel. To go to university. To study Nietzsche and history, Eliot and Che Guevara.

Wayne started to peel the purple skin from the onion, layer by layer.

'His references to your mother made me think about that other story we've got—the original letter.'

I remained silent.

'Maybe we've been looking at this all wrong.' Shaking his hands free of onion skin, he drew me in under his chin and spoke gently.

'What if, in fact, Enid has been telling the truth all this time? What if your father really was a policeman? Do you need to go back and take a second look?'

'Perhaps.' I nodded. 'Worth a shot, for sure. But what I still don't get is why, Wayne? If the story about him working for the IRA is true, why did she run away with someone like him? It doesn't make sense. She seems to have been so smart.' An unfamiliar sense of pride made me pause.

'So why did she head off with a criminal, on a journey to who knows where?' I turned away from him, fussing with the tomatoes.

'Yeah ... in some ways she and I are alike. But I would never have done what she did.' Scraping the block of parmesan back and forth across the grater, I looked up and caught the half-sad, half-quizzical look my lover threw me.

In some way, I'd managed to upset him.

He kept chopping the onions and refused to meet my eyes. Finally, he responded. 'Character might be inherited, as you suggest. Remember the way you were when I first met you? Such an intelligent woman, I thought, but so insecure about the way she looks. About her sense of place in the world. You're still unaware of how beautiful I find you.'

He made me colour crimson. And my unasked questions vanished into the night. He lay the knife on the bench and dragged me into his arms again.

'When I look at you, I see your strong soul and I see a gorgeous woman. I love you. And I knew how much I loved you very early on. Remember when I tried to tell you how beautiful you were, and you used to back away?'

I squeezed my eyes shut. Buried my face into his shoulder and clung to him.

'I think Enid was the same. Everyone we've talked to so far remembers how beautiful Margaret was. And how homely Enid was.'

He pushed me back from him, giant hands clamped on my shoulders.

'You're Enid's daughter in that respect, Suz. She was insecure. She was unsure of herself. She felt like a disappointment to others. That's part of the reason she left with your father. He was probably very charming.'

Wayne turned away, up-ended the onions into the skillet and scraped the knife across the wooden board, ensuring all the little bits made it into the pan.

'This is, of course, assuming the letter *is* the truth,' I reminded him. 'But let's say it is. What do I do now?'

'Well, I for one am tired of the past hanging over our heads,' he said. 'This week at work I did some research.' Garlic sizzled in the shallow frying pan. 'There's a police association you can contact in Victoria. They hold the records of past coppers and if enough time has passed—fifty years, I believe—anyone can access the information. Suz, you just need to supply a name, a date of birth, and the time frame when you think your father worked in the force.

'You can use the letter Enid wrote to you for the dates. Use the two names she gave. The embargo might be the reason why you never found out anything when you first went looking. You looked for a Gerald O'Connor before, a Murphy, but we've never revisited this idea. And it was so many years ago. Enid did say he was using an alias, so how would you have ever found him anyway? Maybe we've ignored the obvious. Do you need to go back and take a second look? If it means we can look forward instead of back, then I'm all for it.'

8

Dubbo, November 2012

> *Dear Miss Hull,*
>
> Thank you for your email in regard to a former member of the Victoria Police.
>
> The closest match we can find is that of a Gerald Sean O'Connor, 66574 . . .
>
> We are pleased to enclose for your perusal a copy of Mr O'Connor's index card and his record of conduct and service . . . The information on file at the museum is past the 40-year embargo limit . . .

I sat wide-eyed in my bedroom, Millie snoring against the small of my back. I was reading and rereading the pages one after the other, scattering them across the bed only to pick them up again in random order. His name, his date of birth, height, eye colour and religion all matched with the information Enid had given in her original letter to me.

RECORD
A scribbled out *'Single'* was replaced with *'Married, 11.2.53'*. (The wife he abandoned for Enid.)

'Gained No. 9 place out of 18 recruits tested. Well conducted. Possesses some natural ability. Needs to apply himself to his duties in a more diligent manner. Obtained Unigrip certificate, Bronze Medallion and Cross, and award of merit for swimming.' Sgt P.B. Morel.

'3.9.54. I commend Constable O'Connor 66574 for zeal and ability displayed in the execution of his duty, which resulted in the conviction of two persons for larceny as servants.' Sgt P.B. Morel.

'22.5.58. Commended with three others for careful and intelligent enquiries and devotion to duty displayed in the apprehension and conviction of a man for larceny of cars.' Sgt. J.W. Hill.

'4.8.59. Commended with six others for excellent investigations which resulted in the detection and conviction of a dangerous criminal for wounding with intent to murder.' Sgt. J.W. Hill.

'30.11.59. Unreliable and untruthful.'

'Date of leaving Force—15.12.59. Resignation for personal reasons.'

I lingered long over that date in November, in 1959; what had he done? But I knew this information was as close as I'd come to uncovering who my father was. Still, it took me days to accept that Enid's letter was the truth.

Wayne was even more cautious. At the end of that week, he lumbered into the house, three or four grocery bags clutched in each hand. This was his self-appointed task on the way home from the mine. He loved scanning the supermarket shelves and surprising me with new varieties of cheese or smoked salmon, or the latest type of stuffed olives.

'Do you still want to meet him, Suz?' he questioned, utterly serious. 'It's fair to assume that because all this is true,' and he indicated the paperwork from Victoria cluttering the table, 'that everything else Enid said about him is also true.

'That means, sweetheart, that somewhere in Victoria you have more half-sisters or brothers. Somewhere in Western Australia this man may still be alive. Under an alias, possibly.' And gently, 'What about his criminal past? That mark on his record? Raising money for the IRA? Is he someone you really want to know?'

Wayne collapsed into a kitchen chair, pulled me down into his lap, held me close to him.

'If you want this, you know I'll support you. I've always got your back, Suz. If you decide to stand up for yourself and face this old skiv, then I'm with you a hundred per cent. We can drive across to Perth, no worries. It'll only take a few days. But I need you to think, my girl. And make up your mind for certain. We've got plans and I don't want anything to get between us and what we want.'

Sitting on my husband's lap, our kitchen filled with bountiful food, a weak sun shining through the windows, I truly believed all I had to do was meet up with my father and fill in missing details of those last days of his relationship with Enid. Then I would know who I was. The past would connect with the present. All the big questions in my life would be finished with. That's what I honestly believed.

The next day, my search started all over again—I was back tracing the mythical Irishman.

Rifling through Google and the online archives of Melbourne newspapers, I looked for the wedding date identified in the police record. I hoped to find a wedding notice or, if I was lucky, a society page with a picture of them.

The black-and-white photograph was on page nine in one of the local rags. On the eleventh day of February, 1953, Gerald Sean O'Connor, police officer, married Kathleen Mary Daley.

The picture showed him—outfitted in his dark police uniform— assisting his new wife, with outstretched hand, into a car. His face was turned away from the camera but she was caught in profile, slight and lovely, a crown of white flowers on her head, her dress a glorious bell of creamy lace. The report noted they were attended by his best man, John Terence Browne, a fellow officer from North Melbourne.

There was a well-rounded number of ten J. Brownes in North Melbourne. Three out of the first five attempts rang out. One old man who answered his phone had no idea who I was talking about, and the other had only recently moved to Melbourne.

Number six on the list was the winner!

And as it turned out, Mr Browne still had the telephone number for Mary. She was the daughter O'Connor had left behind in Melbourne when he ran away with Enid. Mary—my other half-sister.

'I've discovered that my father is a man called Gerald O'Connor,' I said to Mary cautiously over the phone. 'I was adopted, you see. In 1961. And I think that perhaps you and I might be related.' Pausing for a breath, I doodled on the page in front of me. 'If we could establish that fact, maybe you could tell me how to get in contact with him?'

On the other end of the phone, Mary let out a long breath. 'Wow!' and she laughed a little nervously.

'Susan, is it?'

'Yes.' And I explained my long and complicated story to her.

In response, Mary was generosity itself. Warm and friendly. She told me that her father lived in Perth, under an alias. She explained the circumstances in which she'd last seen him, why she wasn't in contact with him anymore—and why she didn't trust him and nor should I.

That afternoon, the warmth between this sister and I issued smooth and easy. We understood each other from the very first phone call, and we still maintain a close relationship today. Mary was the person who gave me the final piece in the puzzle. Without her, I would never have found the Irishman.

Later that night, she emailed me our father's address in Perth—and his phone number.

9

Perth, July 2013

TWELVE MONTHS LATER, ON THE 5th of July, Wayne and I were standing in the central business district of Perth outside Durty Nelly's Irish Pub. This was where we'd arranged to meet my birth father, but a tour group was blocking the entrance to the hotel. We couldn't even make it through the front doors.

'This is the exact opposite of what your father said, Suz,' Wayne muttered under his breath, trying to steer me from behind through the herd. 'Quiet, my eye. It's going to be impossible to find him in there.'

And it seemed to be true. Even after we'd ploughed our way into the timbered hallway, I couldn't see a thing. Most people towered over me. Bodies were jammed up next to each other. Seeing beyond whoever was directly in front of me, or beside me, was impossible. After coming so close, after waiting so long, was I to be cheated out of all the answers I needed?

The Irish Rovers played through the loudspeakers, but the music was barely discernible, and the bar an unreachable land mass across an ocean of heads. I dismissed the notion of grabbing a table, let alone ordering and eating lunch.

I turned a hundred and eighty degrees, ending up back against the solid force of my lover's middle, and lifted my face to mouth words at him.

'This is dreadful,' I said, and he nodded in agreement, eyes copperhead hard.

'He did this on purpose, didn't he?' I mumbled.

Wayne caught my words, though he didn't need to hear them because he was thinking the same thing. With his help, one hand clamping my elbow, the other gripping the straps of my backpack, we inched in the other direction, towards the beer garden. Then a space opened up ahead of me.

A pause in time, a shaft of sky—and I saw him. A familiar face between me and the outside bar; something in his expression that I recognised. Lines scrawled on his forehead like unfinished poetry.

The old man identified me in the same instant and his eyes asked, his mouth shaped, a question that didn't need to be spoken or heard. I pulled urgently on Wayne's hand till he understood. Though we were beyond shouting distance, my father and I managed to communicate the arrangement—to move towards a corner. As Wayne and I circumnavigated some dining tables, a young couple stood up abruptly and I dived in so fast that no one else had a second's chance to own those seats.

Wayne remained standing, motioning to the timeworn man who was now balancing three beers in two hands.

The swell of the crowd got louder. I raised my head, watching Gerald O'Connor walk towards me. I reminded myself that what he knew was also mine to know.

O'Connor set the beers down with expert ease, shook Wayne's hand, leaned across and kissed me on one cheek then the other, his bony fingers gripping me tight.

He slid on to the bench seat next to me. He was diminutive and watchful. In that moment, I recalled everything Enid and Mary had said about this Irishman. But most of all I remembered Mary's remarks about his slyness—his charisma. Why I shouldn't trust him. I could see it immediately. He wore charm easily: like his cheap suit.

Blue eyes deeply set in his face, a pointed chin, overdressed for such a warm day in clothes that were easily thirty years old. Wayne later said to me that the old man had obviously been trying to look respectable, but to his mind, it made him seem like even more of a skiv.

O'Connor turned towards me, measured me up. Leisurely he examined my face, studied my figure, and the initial words he spoke in his Irish brogue affirmed everything.

'Well, darlin', I think you're a mite too pretty to be any daughter of mine. Aye, to be sure. No father could be so lucky as to own such a fine thing as yourself. I bet you make all the boys crazy with that little figure of yours.'

His gaze shifted across to Wayne, who was sitting on the opposite side of the table. 'Or any fella. I bet she makes you one very happy man. Know what I mean?' And I missed it because in embarrassment I had lowered my eyes, but Wayne told me later that the old man had winked at him.

I had to shout, which was somewhat undignified. It was difficult to stand your ground, argue your point, when you could barely be heard.

'Mr O'Connor, I believe I'm your natural daughter.'

He remained silent for longer than I expected, and scrutinised my face again.

'That might just be possible, my little darlin'. Indeed.'

I ran my fingers along the back of my neck, under the collar of my shirt. I glimpsed Wayne's impassive face and decided to not linger.

I braced my spine against the seat. Glanced sideways at the old man.

'I'd like to ask you some questions, Mr O'Connor. If that's okay?'

'To be sure,' he said. Then he asked me to call him by his other name—his alias. I decided to call him nothing. I dug my hand into the bowl of raw peanuts. Started to snap the shells apart.

'You admit you were in Newcastle in 1961? With Enid? That you were there?'

He dropped his eyes from my face for a second, but then he nodded.

'That would be true. We left Melbourne sometime in 1959. Enid was keen to leave ... err, certain problems behind. I had to get away too. But I didn't ask her to come with me. She just kind of turned up.'

He peered at me again, took a slug of his Guinness. He was edging in too close to me, but because of the roar of the crowds, I allowed it. Not only did I need to hear what he said, I also wanted to understand the nuances in his voice, the subtle emphasis, negative or positive, of his tales of ignorance or deceit.

I felt unnatural in his presence—and uncomfortable. Very much on edge. I intuitively understood that it was important to hide my true self, and my motivations for being there. He seemed like the kind of person who, if he knew I wanted something badly, such as information about my past, might withhold it.

'On my original birth certificate,' I stated, 'Enid is named as my natural mother. It also says I was born in Newcastle, in May 1961. The same time you were there with her.' Slipping the stiff paper out of the backpack crammed between my knees, I smoothed out the document on the wooden table between us.

'You said in your letter last month that you didn't even know she was pregnant?'

But the old charlatan wasn't caught that easily. He wagged a finger in my face.

'No. I knew. She and me rowed about it.' He rubbed the side of his long nose. 'But she told me she'd got it seen to.'

I shook my head, suddenly furious, indicating with a gesture, with both hands, that I was alive and healthy.

'How could you misunderstand such a situation? The relationship between you and my mother wasn't exactly platonic. You must have noticed the physical changes?'

'Well . . .' He gazed at Wayne again. Ignored me.

'Enid was a keen woman,' he said, and this time I saw the wink. I concentrated on flattening out the birth certificate with both my hands. For as long as I'd possessed it, I'd been unable to force the creases out.

'You do look like her, love,' O'Connor said.

Nodding, I began to wonder if perhaps the old man was going senile. Which position was he arguing? Was he agreeing he was my birth father or not?

'I know. But I look like you, too, I think.'

The similarity was too plain for him to deny.

'And that be grand. And if you are my daughter, darlin', well that would be a proud day for any man.'

Sipping at my own Guinness, I realised that senile or not, he was clever enough to not once, straight up, admit his paternity. He was running a middle line. He seemed lonely enough to entertain the idea of a long-lost daughter, but too worried about his pot of gold to admit responsibility.

'Enid wrote me a letter. She claimed you two spent another couple of years travelling around Australia after I was born in Newcastle.'

He laughed.

'Hang on, darlin'. First, we went up the coast to Sydney. Then we spent another year in Newcastle. Afterwards, we hopped across to Alice. Hunkered down there for three months, maybe longer.' He counted up on his fingers. 'Then Darwin. Katherine. Perth. She stayed, maybe, for another twelve months. Then I came home from the club one night and she'd bolted. Left no word, nuthin'.

'What else you want to know, love?'

I squeezed my hand into a fist under the table. Jammed it into the wood.

'Enid said you were raising money for the IRA?'

'That's right,' he agreed readily. 'Doin' my bit for the cause back home.'

I took a breath, and for the first time in hours my lungs expanded properly.

'But exactly how'd you do it? What did you do? I didn't even know the IRA were active in Australia.'

'Oh, it was easy enough, darlin'. A quiet tap on the right man's shoulder in the pub at night. Fixing the nags. I arranged fundraisers and suchlike.'

'And the alias? Why'd you start using another name?'

'Well, I got into a bit of trouble in Newcastle. Was too danger-ous to use my old name afterwards. The cops were after me 'cos of what I'd done, and raising money for the cause wasn't looked on too kindly. The coppers in Melbourne, too. They wanted me because of my wife.' His chin started to wobble. He swallowed a long draught of beer. 'There was other strife as well.'

I pressed him. 'What kind of strife?'

'Well, me takings were low. Too low.' He cleared his throat.

'I got word the boys weren't happy.' His hands started to shake. 'So, I went for the big bucks. Didn't work out right, truth be told. No one was meant to get hurt.' He brought his glass to his mouth. Took another long swallow.

'Anyway, I've said too much, darlin'. Just keep it all under your hat. The past should be left in the past.' He shot me a nervous look.

I shifted my glance across to Wayne and signalled with my eyes. I could not bear another second with this man.

'Well, it's time we should be leaving. We need to get back to the hotel and get ready to leave.'

His bleary eyes lifted and he seized my free hand in his.

'If you were my baby, Susannah,' I noticed he used a variation of my name for the first time, 'well that would make me a proud dad.' He dropped his hand to the table. Silence lurched between the three of us. Then my father decided to share one more thing.

'There was talk you know, Susannah.'

I glanced at him.

'There was talk that Enid was up the duff with another baby. That she gave him away too. When she got back to Melbourne.' My father paused—in what seemed a carefully crafted way. 'Maybe, when you get home, you can ring me again? We've got a lot of catching up to do.'

Curiosity flared up in my gut. A brother? I looked at Wayne. Maybe the search wasn't over just yet! But the face that met mine in the pub that day looked tired. My darling man was about done with all this. His eyes were flat as they met mine. I knew right then I had to choose: the past or the present? I brushed my father's fingers off my leg and decided—I chose the truth Wayne had been trying to drum into me since we'd met—there was only now.

We exited the pub with great relief, breathed in fresh air, and decided to walk the city. I rubbed at my hands like a demented Lady Macbeth, shook free my hair. I wanted to leave my father and my hereditary background behind me in that pub. It was an easy choice to make. He wasn't who I was. Neither he nor Enid had anything to do with me. It was time to leave old history behind and move forward with Wayne.

By chance, the return to our accommodation later that evening passed by the Durty Nelly, through Shafto Lane. The tall office blocks reflected the light of the dying sun; the night was closing in. Shivering in the sudden chill, I folded my denim jacket tighter about my body. And there, ahead of us, O'Connor was wandering in that tentative, vague way men get when they're pissed but are trying to appear sober. He'd remained drinking. Alone, he was tottering down the hill into a growing dusk. He was unaware of our presence and we kept our distance till he disappeared from view.

My final image of my father then was of a solitary old man, stumbling away from his one opportunity to acknowledge the truth and create a relationship with his daughter. He was trapped in his lies. The past had ambushed him and eaten him whole. He was a friendless drunk in an out-of-date suit sacrificing me, and his integrity, to preserve his darkest secrets. That day I truly understood how an unacknowledged past could mess up somebody's present. The fear of revealing his history to me, the fear of revealing who he'd once been, was a more powerful influence over my father than the chance to love and hold the child he'd produced.

On reflection, Enid's life too had been profoundly affected, in a very similar way. Keeping her secrets about her two little baby Susans was, I imagined, an anxiety that gnawed at her every day.

Meeting my birth mother and father demonstrated to me one very important truth: the secrets we hold onto make us very vulnerable.

Part 2

Finding Love

2014–2015

10

Country New South Wales, December 2014

IT SEEMED IT HAD ALL been for nothing.

I was disappointed in who my father was and disappointed in how nothing appeared to have changed within me—that there had been no great shifting of ground within my soul. After such a crazy journey halfway around Australia, all the years of emotional turmoil, nothing was apparently different. Two supposed fathers, two sisters, and a whole lot of mixed-up stories. Was I any closer to finding *me*? It didn't feel like it.

By the end of 2014, my sense of self had been reduced to a handful of confetti someone had hurled into the air—it rained down in pieces around me.

Yet there was one large, beautiful distraction who made the letting go of an unsatisfactory search for identity simple for me: Wayne. He loved me. I belonged to him. We were connected. We were together and we had a future.

We'd spent much of the intervening year and a half since the trip to Perth organising the dream we'd always shared—a year away in southern Spain: to bask in the Andalusian sun, shop at the local markets, enjoy a stolen lifetime together somewhere exotic. We would drink Rioja, read Hemingway, learn to speak Spanish. We would challenge ourselves in an unfamiliar place, travel whenever the whim directed us. Both of us were dying for the romance and the thrill of it all.

I decided I was ready to embrace the mantra he'd been repeating to me all along: the past is insignificant, live in the moment, there is only now. I prepared to leave for Spain believing everything the man I loved had always told me.

It was late afternoon and we were watching a storm as it moved across the horizon. The sky was ponderous with rain. There were two days left before we were due to leave Australia. Our new life was about to begin.

We'd spent the morning finishing our packing: choosing what to throw away, what to box up into storage and leave at Wayne's mother's, and what to take with us. Load after load of my furniture had been piled into the ute to give to friends or to drag to the dump. Now, Wayne sipped a beer while I sat with my back supported against the blistering, hot house, nibbling an orange picked from a tree in the garden. The going away card my students had given me lay on the veranda, half trapped beneath my sunburnt thigh.

The wind started up, brushing leaves off the trees in the front yard. Sheep being run on the bone-dry creek bed opposite the house nosed the thorns in the dirt. I could hear the nicker of an anxious pony along the dirt road.

Wayne pulled me towards him, pulling me in under his shoulder. His size and the touch of his hands on my flesh always grounded me. His solidity made me feel more substantial.

'I can't believe in a few days we'll be gone from here forever,' I said. We had no idea where we would live when we returned, although Wayne had spoken vaguely of us retiring to the Queensland hinterland. Teaching had been important to me. Leaving my friends and family wasn't as easy as I'd thought it would be. I was a jumble of emotions.

'Suz. Be happy. You've raised Jonno right. He's independent, he's been living his own life for years. He loves Sydney. And I know your mum hasn't much time left but she's well cared for. You've given ten years of effort to the kids you've taught. And finally, you've got the answers you were looking for.' He kissed the top of my head. 'And me? I've spent my whole life looking after my family, my brothers, my sisters. I've worked hard. It's time for us.'

I bent his fingers back one by one, listened for the crack, tried to concentrate on what he was saying and what I wanted to say in return.

'It's all connected though, don't you think? Aren't we a product of all those experiences?'

He shook his head. 'I think about it in a different way.' His words sounded powerful in the silence before the storm.

'Living in the now? Einstein didn't believe in it—he thought our present, our future, our past, all occurred simultaneously. I don't agree with that. I believe we can make our own version of time. If we choose to.' He rested his chin on the top of my head, taking his time to work through his thoughts.

'We need to be aware of every single moment we're experiencing, right this minute ... because there is only now. Forget the past! Conscious choices about the present have to be made, or we hold onto what's happened before and that becomes who we are.'

He tilted my face up to his. 'Remember I told you, when we first met, about my old man?' I struggled out of his arms and twisted around to better watch his expression. I tried to mask the surprise I imagined was spreading across my face. He never talked about his father. He looked at me for a long moment.

'When I was younger, I let those experiences with him define me. I was afraid I would turn out like him. That what he did, what I did, would mark me for life. The devil's mark.' He turned his head and stared out at the Macquarie River.

'Then one day, I realised that if I didn't stop thinking about my past it would ruin me. By making that single decision I became stronger, Suz. The past must be buried and remain buried—otherwise it kills you.'

I nodded.

'I want you to forget about the adoption. Your biological parents. Make an agreement with me that this year we will simply live each hour as it happens.'

I nodded again; it seemed so important to him, and by then I was willing to give him anything he asked for.

Because on that day, and on so many other days, Wayne was a real-life hero to me. He was the kind of man I'd dreamt about—but the kind of man I never thought would love me: the plain, plump, bookish little girl who felt like she never fitted in. I thought his kind of man was out of my league. He was Darcy, Mr Rochester; he was Antony. He was 'my North, my South'. He was the wild kid from New Guinea with the dramatic upbringing who'd read Graham Greene. He was intelligent, strong, handsome and complicated. Despite his occasional criticism about how I was too 'soft', too 'emotional', we were happy and content in one another's company.

When I told him that afternoon about Aristophanes' theory of love, he seized it with both hands, certain we were the embodiment of the cartwheeling couple joined as one. Wayne believed we had each found our other half, and he convinced me of it too.

This man was secure in his footing on the earth. I loved that strength and that certainty about him. I loved how we fitted together so easily. I loved that he loved me. That this was the man I was travelling to Spain with made the world more miraculous. My happiness was secured, my future guaranteed. Love. Travel. Adventure. All the good things in the world were finally mine. So, I set aside my misgivings about what he was saying, about forgetting the past, and instead fixed my mind on us being together.

He gulped down the last of his beer. The dust was beginning to lift off the dirt road and drops of rain had commenced their assault on our tin roof. It was time to go in. We needed to pack up the kitchen utensils, defrost the fridge and wrap Mum's good china in newspaper. The world that day smelt fresh, green and full of promise.

11

Sydney Airport Hotel, early January 2015

IT WAS 8 P.M. AND both of us were too wired to sleep.

'What's the thing you regret most about leaving home?' I asked him as I sat at the desk in the hotel room, tapping at the keyboard of my laptop, keen to busy myself. The excitement about tomorrow was almost unbearable.

'Nothing.' He swivelled in his chair by the window, away from the view of the planes. 'I didn't ever expect my life would turn out like this. That I would be doing this. When I met you, I was just expecting to meet a lady to go out to dinner with.'

I grinned, used to this recollection. 'Okay, so what's the thing you are most looking forward to in Granada?'

And he didn't miss a beat. 'Being with you.'

He leant forward in the chair, eyes on my face. 'What are you doing? Are you working on your book?'

'Kind of. It's just some ideas. About what it feels like to be leaving home for such a long time, what it feels like to be flying into the unknown, with just you by my side.' I grinned. 'What it's like to finally be loved and to belong to someone.'

'I do love you, Suz. You know how much. Never forget it.' Then he gave a kind of half grin. Kind of teasing. 'Hope not too much of this book is going to be about me?'

I shook my head at him over the open lid of the laptop, my fingers resting on the keyboard.

'Of course some of it has to be about you. You've changed my life.'

An emotion I couldn't identify swept across his face. Then he turned away, back to the large picture window, to watch the planes taking off and landing from runways lit by a pattern of confusing neon lights.

Wheedling, I changed the subject. 'Right now, I'm just concentrating on what it feels like to be leaving everybody behind. I'm trying to catch that sensation.'

Next morning, Wayne lugged most of the suitcases—holding everything we imagined we would need for the next twelve months—out the hotel door. I dragged the remaining luggage behind me, following him. Looking back, we were undertaking an extraordinary gamble. When we returned to Australia, there would be no jobs waiting for us. There'd be no four walls to call home. The sum total of our belongings, including Millie—currently lodged at Wayne's mother's farm—would fit into Wayne's car: a whittled down collection of books, art, music, photos, the dog and some paperwork—just the significant stuff.

From then on, we only had each other to rely on. Honestly, I couldn't wait.

12

Somewhere across the Indian Ocean, January 2015

WAYNE WAS A POWERFUL MAN, but terribly shy in some ways. I believed his shoulders were so broad because of the lifetime he'd spent carrying the burden for others. He'd told me numerous times that Papua New Guinea was no longer the place he remembered. And because his father had made his childhood so harsh, I understood this to be the reason he chose not to discuss the first twenty-five years of his life. All the time he was with me I believed this to be a point of honour for him.

There were indicators, besides his occasional use of Pidgin, that revealed his unconventional background—no matter how much he didn't want to talk about it. And I treasured those marks in my heart. I loved him for both his traditional qualities of manhood and for those differences about him.

One difference was his accent. Wayne had a deep baritone voice and appeared oblivious to the influences of inflection from the Dutch and Germanic people who'd populated New Guinea while he was growing up. And if his height, demeanour and general broad build weren't enough to inspire intimidation, the accent always sealed the deal. What others saw was a man who held authority easily. In all our time together, he was invariably the alpha male in any room we entered. Rightly or wrongly, I loved him for that, too.

Sometimes, in his pronunciation of words, there was an old-fashioned distinction. When he used the word 'says' he always rhymed it with 'days' instead of rhyming it with 'fez', as I did. Casual table manners too, evidence of his upbringing by his father. He ate fast, with glee, but rarely held his knife or fork in the 'proper' way, as I'd been taught. Sometimes I had to bite back middle-class rebukes about 'slowing down' or 'using cutlery'. I never could understand his rather obsessional attitude towards food.

Blowing his nose or wiping his hands was always done using one of those massive cotton handkerchiefs my own father had used. He neatened his hair with a round plastic comb, similar to one my grandfather had owned.

I loved him for all these things; they seemed to symbolise the heart of his masculinity.

Somewhere across the Indian Ocean, he reached over the armrest and tried to smooth down some strands of my hair, rising about my face due to the open air-conditioning vents. I gave him a look and he shrugged.

'I can't keep my hands off you.'

I was reading the book about New Guinea that he always believed best explained the first expedition by white men into the interior: *The Sky Travellers*.

'Are you honestly enjoying it?' One arm was draped across my knee, sneakily dragging me closer to him. 'Or have I pushed you into reading this book, Suz, when you didn't want to? I like it because it's the first time both black and white are given a voice. In print.'

I turned the book face down on my lap and stretched both hands to capture his.

'I love it! Seriously, I do.' I fiddled with his square fingers, trying to quell my curiosity.

'I admit, the unfamiliar names of places confuse me at times. I can't keep all the names straight in my head. But I'm enjoying it.' I paused for a breath.

'Anyway, how can I *not* be interested and excited about this book? It's about the place where you grew up.'

By way of response, he folded my cotton skirt, pleat by deliberate pleat, away from my knees, his hand searching for bare skin. Then he returned his eyes to the window, leant forward to catch a glimpse of the ocean below, and was silent.

For once, I decided to push him. I mean, why had he given me the book to read if he didn't want me to ask questions?

'Look. I know we agreed not to talk about your past. But just tell me one story about what it was like growing up in the Highlands, Wayne. Please?'

He frowned. Crossed his arms. But I kissed him on the cheek. 'C'mon, just one story. Then I promise, promise, I will never ask you another single thing.'

He relented. He told me a story about when he was a 'piccaninny'—living near Goroka in the Highlands of Papua New Guinea—the day he and his brother John had discovered the violence of the place, right on their doorstep.

'I was five or six years old at the time, and our timber house backed up against the banana trees. The housekeeper, a woman my father had flown up from country New South Wales, was always worried about the snakes.

'At the front of the house, there was a large field, about the size of a football field, where the villagers held a market on the weekend.

'While he was skinning the chicken, the houseboy had told my father that an important battle was being organised between two tribes. All the warriors were filing down from the mountains. We heard the servants chattering about it for days.

'John and I were on the veranda the day it happened—we were so small we couldn't even see over the wooden railing properly. We took turns at trying to boost each other up.' He smiled at the memory.

'One of the men, who worked for my father, stole a sledge-hammer out of the shed behind the house. He was going to use it in the fight. My father saw what the man had done and thought it was unfair. So, he strode through the middle of that crowd—there were thousands of men—to seize his sledgehammer back.

'You should've seen it. The men were leaping up and down in warrior dress. Bows were clutched in their hands. Arrows shooting across the sun. The noise was thunderous. Drums beating. Colours flashing. The stamping. All I could smell was crushed pineapple. And blood. But because my father wasn't part of the fight, the men let him take the sledgehammer back without attacking him. That column of furious men simply separated in half.

'See, my father had a reputation. Both blacks and whites feared him, and respected us boys because of it. He was the first in the Highlands to run a fuel-carting business. Across the mountains.' Wayne turned his eyes back to the window; took his time; took a breath.

'He was tough, my father. He used to beat me black-and-blue because I wouldn't call his partner "mother". My father believed he was lord and *Masta* over everyone. That day, after he retrieved his property, the local police cordoned the area off so the men could get on with it. There were twenty-five killed that day—most of them trampled in the swelling dust. I just remember the black skin. And a noise that grew louder and louder.'

I squeezed his hand.

'John and I would take turns at running away, at hiding in the jungle. But people were so afraid of my old man, they repeatedly returned us.' He grinned. 'Didn't stop us, though.'

Then his face grew more serious.

'Mum made one desperate journey to Australia, before she and my father officially separated, hoping she could escape Stan, hoping she could get us kids away from the old man. I was seven. John, five. But in Sydney, Mum was tricked by my father's sister.' Wayne rubbed the bridge of his nose. 'We thought, Mum thought, that we were just being taken out for the afternoon. For ice cream. Anyway, my aunt bundled both of us boys onto a plane and . . .' My husband shrugged and stared out the window again. 'Basically, we were kidnapped—taken back to Goroka and back to my father.'

'Afterwards, Mum returned to Port Moresby and waited for a divorce. But the old man was powerful. She remained for years down there. I didn't see her till I was a grown man.'

He must have seen my stricken face. 'But it wasn't all bad. My idols when I was a teenager were writers like Kipling, le Carré, Chandler. My father hated me reading so I'd devour them in secret, in the cab of a truck, up the mountain somewhere or by a campfire, when I was supposed to be asleep. I loved that road and that mountain, even though we were working hard. The adventures John and I had together up there!'

The fullness in his voice aroused my love. I was overwhelmingly sorry for that little boy—and at the same time I respected the individual who, after such a difficult life, had emerged to become the man sitting beside me. I decided on that day not to ask him any more questions about his time in New Guinea.

'How can I be in a relationship with you? *And* be flying to Spain, to spend a perfect twelve months? It makes me a little afraid. I can't believe our good luck.'

My pulse quickened, with a shiver of fear. It seemed almost *too* good to be true—the way things were working out for us both.

Wayne shrugged. 'There is no evidence of a benevolent god, Suz. No evidence of a god at all. We control our destiny for a moment— if we're lucky.' Behind him, captured through the porthole, I saw blue sky. 'So, we need to grab that moment now. Not regret what will come about in the future to make us pay for it. This is our year! A timeless space between the past and the future.'

13

Granada, January 2015

OUR NEW SPANISH HOME WAS near the top of a mountain. It was part of a row of traditional two-storey terrace houses built directly underneath the Palace of Alhambra, in the old Jewish quarter, the Realejo of Granada. The houses faced directly onto a terraced walkway with one of the finest views of the city. Even on that first day we could hear the legendary nightingales in the trees above us, nesting in the forest of English elms that surrounded the castle.

Wayne, following the instructions we'd been sent, drew out an old-fashioned key ring from under a watering can in front of a set of French doors. He unlocked the main door and, inside the hallway, the door leading into our apartment. We abandoned our luggage on the pavement and dashed into our new place like teenagers.

The first thing that caught my eye was a large print by Matisse, hung on a dividing wall between the sitting room and what I imagined to be our bedroom.

Wayne grinned wolfishly at me, 'How appropriate.'

I grinned back. 'It's a sign.'

Both of us understood exactly what the other was thinking: this was our year of freedom—the personal pilgrimage we were making to pleasure. That *La Danse* hung on the wall of our new home seemed most fitting.

The room was beautifully simple. It was painted bright white, and the French doors were positioned against the external wall to capture the view of Granada and let in the light. But for now, the window remained firmly shut against the face of a freezing Spanish winter. In the corner sat a small stove and a fridge. The shelves held a few pieces of cutlery, glassware, a saucepan.

My husband turned serious, wandering from the living room into our bedroom, inspecting every inch of the apartment. There was an ensuite bathroom beyond the bedroom. This room was at the very rear of the house and the back wall was built directly against the cliff.

'This will do just fine, Suz. Three rooms are plenty enough.' He kissed me again in the narrow space between the sink and the large, concrete bath. I slung my arms around his neck, melted into his big body.

'You're shivering again, love.'

'Yeah, it's *so* cold. I can't believe how cold it is. I never expected it. But I've never felt this excited either, Wayne. We're so lucky, aren't we?'

Later, after he coaxed the heater into life, we began dragging in our mishmash of luggage. But my husband said, 'Go take a bath—warm up, love. I'll take care of this.' As I soaked chin high in the hot water, he shouted through the doorway that it had started to snow! It was the first time he'd ever seen it and I could hear the excitement in his voice. I bounded out of the tub and dragged a towel about myself. I wanted to see it, too! I heard the creak of the front door as he pushed it open, the slushy sound as he stepped outside. Dripping all over the floor, I stared through the French doors as he wandered across the terrace to the edge of the gorge, lifting his head to gaze up at the night sky. The flakes fell straight down and settled thickly on the shoulders of his black coat.

Later, we teetered our way through soft piles of snow to make it down to town. In the frozen stillness of night, we became disoriented, but we weren't worried. We had hours. And no bags this time! No place to be. I held fast to my husband's hand. The trip down was much easier than the trip up earlier in the day.

When we finally reached street level, he leant down and kissed the back of my neck. At the kerb we looked both ways, alert to the danger of traffic moving in the opposite direction to Australia—but the road was deserted. I tucked my arm through the crook of his elbow and we strolled beneath a line of trees strung with fairy lights, the warm smell of sugared churros floating through the air. And somehow, twenty minutes later, we happened inside a half-lit place called Bodegas Castenada.

I remember the Castenada as a haven of warmth and noise. People were squeezed in so tightly that many had their arms wrapped about the shoulders of the person beside them just to be able to fit. The bar staff shouted across the room to each other through the stink of cigarettes; the chefs sang loudly and out of key while they shoved each other about the kitchen. Crumpled paper serviettes were discarded all over the stone floor, flattened under a hundred pairs of boots. We'd read about this tradition before we'd left home, had expected it, but seeing the nonchalance of it all was glorious. It was all so Spanish!

I glanced about for somewhere to sit, but seats were not an option. Fifty heavy hams, hanging from the ceiling, seemed alive in the yellow light. Covered in a slow-oozing fat, they gleamed like stalactites.

Roaring across dozens of dark heads, Wayne tried out his fledgling Spanish, ordered me *uno vino tinto* and himself *una cerveza grande,* and we propped ourselves at a table by the window, pressed in on all sides. On the far wall, the formidable head of a black bull, stuffed and mounted, hung beside a portrait of Franco.

Our free tapas arrived: a renowned tradition in Granada. You received whatever had been cooked up during the day. In this instance, a plate of shining olives, slivers of sharply scented serrano ham and crusty bread. The waiter scuttled between the drinkers in his black-and-whites, frowning and arguing with everyone. He almost threw our food at us. Each drink, each tapa, made the night more captivating: plump *croquetas de pollo,* stringent *chorizo, tortilla, patatas bravas* coated in thick sweet tomato sauce. I was a light drinker but that night I consumed vast amounts of *vino tinto.* And plate loads of food.

And as we stood, a touch bewildered, within a press of unintelligible language and a fug of smoke, a young couple ventured forward; asked if they could share the stand where we'd planted our drinks.

Ernst and Julia were in their late twenties: she was a lanky beauty from New York, now married to her young Spanish husband; both were residents of Madrid. He coached a first-grade soccer team and she taught English at a secondary school.

'We're here in Granada, 'cos it's where we first met.' Linking her long arms around his neck, she kissed him on the cheek. 'And today it's our anniversary.'

Her Spanish when she translated for him was extraordinary, his English marginal. She towered over the shorter Spaniards, especially the women, and her sweep of golden hair, tied back with a silk scarf tagged by Ralph Lauren, identified her as a foreigner. But she was aware when she spoke—of ethical sensibilities, of national peculiarities. And always she conferred with him, often just with a quick glance, particularly when she was discussing Spanish politics or history. Both of them taught us much.

We learnt, for example, that Spain was a country where 'place' held significant meaning. To be exact, the place where you came from was *most* important. One of the first pieces of information an individual would tell you about themselves was whether they were born in Madrid or Malaga or Cadiz.

Then, the Spanish appellation system contained names from both the mother's and the father's line of heritage—the one double-barrelled surname held 'place' too—through generation after generation.

The other sacred aspect of Spanish identity Julia told us about was the importance of family obligations. The responsibility Spanish families felt towards relatives meant that sometimes sons and daughters literally never left the village or city in which they'd been born.

In the coming months, we witnessed example after example of the old and the new linked together, the connections of past and present. It didn't matter how often we were out on the streets: we always saw family pushing older relatives about in wheelchairs. On Sundays, strolling past the rows of tables set up outside the restaurants for lunch, every generation was represented. Later on in the year, when our landlords disappeared for their summer holidays, all their siblings and both sets of in-laws went with them, too.

The contrast between my recent experiences, discovering my family and my search for 'place', with what we witnessed in Spain seemed a great irony. For a long while I wondered about fate and whether there was some deeper reason why we'd been drawn to this country. Sometimes I admired these ties to family and the past, and at other times I recognised that such strong attachments to kinsfolk, history and tradition might anchor one too firmly.

The most interesting information the couple shared with us that evening was about Franco.

'He is a man,' Ernst explained in his uncertain English, 'who . . .' and he looked to his beautiful wife and chattered in rapid Spanish.

'The trauma of Franco still walks in the memory of many people.' She translated. '"Faith, family and Franco" they would say, back in the day. But neighbours and friends, even brothers and sisters, were sometimes on the opposite political side to each other. One might be a republican, one a nationalist. People were shot or tortured or had their children stolen away because of the neighbours. So now, apparently, everybody agrees that for the purpose of reconciliation, the only thing to do is get on with life. You have to forget the old stuff. You mustn't remember who was a communist or who supported Franco. They're trying to delete history, in a way. For everyone's benefit. These days,' she explained, 'if people speak of Franco, or "*La Guerra*", they speak in whispers.'

'Look,' I interrupted, 'I'm all for trying to live in the present. But this doesn't seem right. You can't just sweep history under the carpet, surely? What about all those people Franco killed? Are they to be forgotten about?'

Julia peeked sideways at her husband. 'It's the only way they can move forward, he says.'

'But you have to understand the reason why things have happened.' I looked at Wayne to back me up, but he was, of course, silent on the subject.

'Everything from your past in some way always affects your present—or your future. If the problem isn't identified and owned, and understood by everybody, then we're all advancing from a false position—we're living a lie. The country will never be whole.

We have this issue in Australia, too. And it's also something I feel very strongly about in terms of my own personal history. You can't keep secrets about the past.'

'Susan,' Wayne said under his breath, tugging at my hand, trying to shush me.

Ernst tried again. Gestured and stumbled over the phrase 'Pact of Forgetting'. His wringing hands indicated his rising frustration at his inability to explain.

'The only way everyone could agree about how to move ahead, how to reconcile both sides of the country, was to bury the past. It was just easier. No one is allowed to speak about that time. Or what it was like for people.'

I raised my eyebrows, but Wayne's fingers tugged on mine again. Despite how inexplicable this attitude seemed to me, one glance at his face and I knew I needed to remain silent about the subject for the rest of the night.

14

Granada, spring 2015

In early May, after spending a month away in Eastern Europe realising our long-held dreams—visiting Prague, Croatia, Austria, Hungary—it was a relief to arrive back in Spain. As wondrous as the experience had been, to leap into a taxi at the airport and immediately understand the driver, to be able to order food and to be able to read signs posted in the street, made us feel, once again, at home. We relaxed. I rang Jonno. Emailed long, happy letters to Di. Updated my Facebook page with photographs from our life in Granada. Made a video for Liz's daughters, Caitlin and Ashleigh, where I showed off our apartment, demonstrating my dreadful Spanish accent. But no matter our massacring of the Spanish language, despite the 'Pact of Forgetting', turning our Australian insides out to adapt to this new and different environment appeared to be working.

Because, a week later, when the Matisse inexplicably fell off the wall, shattering the glass, fragments of it sprinkling in so many directions the apartment blazed in diamonds of afternoon sunlight, we knew exactly where to get it replaced. Thus, naively, I started to believe we'd discovered a new home for ourselves. Believed what little I knew was enough to make me a local! That I was beginning to belong.

'We'll take it to the art place down off the Avenida del Sur,' Wayne said. 'Near the barbers.'

And other things were easier, too. We knew which *supermarcado* to go to for cheap wine. Which bar served the best tapas. Halfway through May, when I was battling a weird skin infection, I learnt I could buy antibiotics straight over the chemist's counter—no doctor's visit required.

'And,' I grinned at Wayne, 'for just three euros, I can get all your old-man medications without needing a new prescription. And it's so cheap!' He grinned back at me as I rushed into the flat, excited because another challenge had been conquered.

'Your blood pressure tablets are less than half the price at home! All we have to do is show the prescription from Australia and the chemist will source the most similar medication he can find from Madrid. Spain is amazing!'

Clothes at the market could be bought for under ten euros, but Wayne hated what he called the tourist 'tat'. I'd lost weight due to all the walking we were doing, so the week before summer officially started, he hustled me down to the Zara on Calle Reyes Catolicos, tugged narrow skirts off the racks, thrust sharply cut jackets at me through the gap in the change room curtains, and encouraged me to imitate the luscious Spanish style.

On the climb home, using his brand-new camera, he posed me standing straight and tall in front of a section of the Alhambra's crumbling honey-coloured wall—hands on hips, face luminous in the early-summer light. For the first time in my life, I believed myself to be beautiful.

Studying the woman in the picture now, I don't recognise her at all.

❀

In addition to us, there were any number of strangers who wanted to call this splendid city home.

The street hippies, for example, who surged in from around the Western world, dwelling in caves in the hills outside town. Loping into the city looking like extras from a Mad Max movie, outfitted in robes of camel-coloured cloth and wearing long plaits of hair, the hippies performed circus tricks to make money to buy food. But for us, lazing in the spring sunshine in the plaza under a red umbrella, Wayne drinking *cerveza grande* and me, *gin y tonica con hielo*, their happy-go-lucky attitude was inspiring. They appeared to live on air.

Bundled up, middle-aged Roma women, *Gitanos,* who haunted the streets, pressing rosemary upon the tourists, pleading with scrunched-up faces, were abided by the rest of the Spanish population and loathed by the holidaymakers. Yet it was their flamenco melodies that we heard, strummed furiously on guitar, floating above the city in the afternoons. The Roma people had created a respected and long-held influence over Andalusian culture, and Granada rang with the sounds of their traditional songs.

The North African refugees desperately attempting to sell umbrellas and fake Gucci handbags on the sidewalks were also tolerated by the Spaniards, to a degree. When the *policia* arrived, it was often Spanish shopkeepers who were the first to kick boxes off the pavement so the refugees could escape.

There seemed to be a beautiful balance. The bourgeois families of Granada met their obligations, laughed a lot, worked tirelessly most hours of the day and articulated their opinions loudly. They feasted daily on fresh *pescado* and drank excellent wine. The Spanish existed in, what appeared to us, to be a permanent state of ebullience; living side-by-side in a city crowded with a complex and diverse set of minorities, everyone crammed tight within the borders of the city. Often, when we were walking the streets, I expected trouble to arise between the many distinct cultures because everybody lived *on* the street. But I never witnessed disputes. Lines of demarcation somehow blurred, or were respected and understood.

'We're in paradise,' I said to Wayne as we relaxed in the shade of the plaza, drinking and watching the daily parade. And for many weeks it had truly felt like that. We were suspended by happiness and a belief that we were untouchable.

The weather was warming up towards one of the hottest summers ever experienced in Southern Spain. The freezing hikes up the steps to our language classes were forgotten, the holiday in Dubrovnik was forgotten, and with our landlords away for a week in Malaga, we made the most of our freedom to drag chairs from the apartment outside and bask in a sunny stupor—idly observing our city, listening to bees buzz through the trees above our heads.

From our front door, we stepped directly onto this shared pavement, bordered by a low wall just several metres away. Tourists would climb the hill up towards the Alhambra, and just before entering the grounds, make a left and lose their way, just like we did that first afternoon, amongst the myriad shadowed alleyways. Before somehow discovering Almanzora Alta. Then they would mill about outside our living room window, gazing over the wall at the city below.

The Spanish call such a space a *mirador*, or in English we might call it a lookout. I would often sit, in the morning, drinking my coffee watching the tourists arrive. If I opened the French doors, I chatted with people from all around the world.

That day, Wayne had heaved the living room chairs through the doorway and arranged them squarely under the orange tree. I hoisted a tray, with a spread, including goat's cheese and cold beer, onto the low wall dividing us from the valley below. The sharp bite of citrus hung in the air.

We didn't care about the extra money it cost to rent the place, or even the gawking tourists so often crowding our path to catch a glimpse of the view. We didn't think about our obvious show of affluence either.

Due to the pressing heat and the glare of mid-afternoon sun, the *mirador* was deserted: tourists pattered about with their selfie sticks elsewhere; the Spanish dozed; even sullen teenagers with stolen bottles of *cerveza* had shifted to cooler spaces. The exception was a Romani man, lying asleep in a patch of hard sunlight. Unfolded across the stones, he lay in front of the neighbours' house, at the end of the *mirador*, where an impenetrable rock wall had been built to impede invaders of old, to protect the Alhambra and the people of Granada. Almanzora Alta was a dead end: one way in and one way out. Unless you fancied climbing over the wall, across the rooftops below and risking a fall into the river.

An expanse of blue sky stretched before us. The sun beat relentlessly on our heads. Across the water, even the tumble of medieval cottages seemed to languish in the heat, beneath terracotta tiles. I slipped my hand together with Wayne's and swallowed the sight— wordless at the beauty of the place. I believed the weight of our luck matched the strength of the heat beating down upon our heads.

For an hour or so we simply sat. We drank.

I remember Wayne leaning over, his shadow blocking the sun, feeding me lumps of goat's cheese; a rosemary twig spiky and sweet against my tongue. Then he disappeared into the kitchen, to grab more beer.

From the corner of my eye I observed the dark-haired Romani stir. When he jumped up, because he wore no shirt, I noticed how terribly thin he was. All bones.

For complicated reasons I struggle to articulate, perhaps in part a sense of guilt at my own good fortune, I stood up and politely waited for him to accustom himself to the light. Then, in an offering I now acknowledge was both patronising and naïve, I stumbled across to him, offering up the platter of tapas with both hands, inviting him in my best Spanish to enjoy the food.

The grateful response I expected was not forthcoming.

Instead, the Romani man danced on the stones, swore at me in a language I couldn't understand. Frightened, I shrugged, and in a display of nonchalance, turned around and flopped back down in my chair. Faced my back to him deliberately. Covered my ears. Watched the doorway of our house.

Then Wayne strode out of the apartment, holding a bottle of San Miguel angled towards his mouth, and I felt my shoulders relax. All was safe now. As he fell into his chair beside me, I shifted over hurriedly and began to explain what had happened. But a sharp pinch to the back of my neck shot me forward. And in a state of confusion, I was half aware of Wayne jerking to his feet and twisting around. In the background, I could hear the other man screaming. Then Wayne hauled me on to my feet. Hauled me away from the wall.

Now everyone stood in open space.

'Go into the house, love,' Wayne muttered.

The stranger's hand then reached between his thighs. Gawking at me, he grasped his dick and began jerking off.

'Get into the house and call the police,' my husband yelled.

Shuffling forward, the man seemed to pitch insults at me while he masturbated. His eyes never left my face. He finished quickly with a 'hah', and wiped his hands down the side of his pants.

Wayne was now crouched low, indicating to the man with his two hands, palms raised, to move back, signalling to him to retreat. All the time ordering me inside.

But I was unwilling to leave. Loyalty drove me—the notion I needed to stand by my man. The two of us had to face this fury together, surely? Plus, I was unsure about Wayne's safety, as immense as he was, against this lithe, tight youth with the intensity of someone possessed.

'Look, my friend. My wife was offering you some food. That's all.'

The man spat twice more. Burned into my brain is the image of a sliver of phlegm glistening on my red, patent leather sandal.

'I am not the animal to be fed in a zoo.' The Romani crossed his arms. 'You live 'ere?' He flashed a hand at the windows of our apartment.

Wayne nodded. Switched automatically back to the Spanish. 'Si.'

Then a glint of silver at the man's hip. I stepped back.

'Your white women smell bad but it has been too long for me. We make a deal. You keep paying out your money to buy my food, my history, my culture. You take everything we are. And I will take this one 'ere.' He extended his arm. With an air of playfulness, he stuck the steel point of the dagger beneath Wayne's chin and feigned swiping sideways. Indicating me.

I twisted my hands together.

But my husband held his ground—cajoling the man. And an aside to me, 'For God's sake, Susan. Get into the house. Now! Call the police! The police! Suz!' I finally heard him. Folded behind him, in through the doorway, stumbled from sunshine into silent shade.

Then a window sash slammed up and a torrent of murderous Spanish thundered down over our heads. It was Senorita Oviedo Perez, from the first-floor flat two doors up. In an instant, the man backed away.

Inside, face blistering with a shame I couldn't quite comprehend, I rested my cheek against the windowpane, listening to the man's last words.

'You come 'ere with all your money made in the big cities else-where. You are like parasites on the dog. But we will not let you buy who we are!'

After that time, the Granada light did not possess the same timeless quality. A threat seemed to be lurking behind every corner. I never did get around to discovering the number to ring in an emergency. Wayne was curiously silent about the incident. Raised his hand at me when I wanted to talk about it.

Perhaps, we brushed away the violent incident too easily. Wayne, eager as ever for the next thing, was curious to see the world he'd never dreamed he'd experience. He was like a boy in the streets, always darting ahead, shouting back over his shoulder, pointing things out to me.

But other places called, too. We decided we would go away again, probably for a month. Maybe more? Wayne missed driving, so the plan was to hire a car and drive north. Up into Galicia, and possibly into France. We planned to finish our journey in Portugal.

Till then, we enjoyed lazy walks through the still, sometimes deserted back streets—long in shadow, overhung by family houses of terraced whitewash. Wayne always bending his tall body in half to leave money in the upturned hats of beggars. Or we would meet new friends for picnics high in Las Alpujarras, on the southern side of the Sierra Nevada; Wayne discussing the Buddhist religion of our Russian friends with them, or the merits of rugby union over soccer. Sometimes it felt like we sat on the grass roof of the world. The mountains unfurled down to the Alboran Sea, across which we could view the plains of Morocco. The sunshine filtered through the cherry blossoms, and daffodils danced beside us. Each day smelled fresh and exciting as the summer progressed.

In the warm murmur of Spanish twilight, in those last few days before we left our fine city, I lay in the bedroom, welcoming my husband, open and wanting, losing myself in him. Our lovemaking joined us physically as one, and if we metaphorically imagined ourselves as Aristophanes' original lovers, the intimacy we enjoyed made the idea a reality. For a little while we were one. With two faces, four legs and four arms. Him, inviolate. Me, pliable and warm. It was the stuff of our dreams.

15

Porto, mid-June 2015

To LEAVE GRANADA, WAYNE, WHO loved to spend the money he'd worked so hard to make, rented the latest-model BMW. It was a big, black, shiny beast that absolutely delighted him. He drove us through central Spain, up through the sunlight of Andorra, into the South of France, humming to himself the entire way. The sound of his happiness had me smiling for days.

One night we stayed in the unconventional city of Montpellier. The next day we were in the car again, travelling between the little villages in the Languedoc region of France. From there, five days later, we crossed back into Spain, climbing across the grand Pyrenees. Wayne stopped the car almost every half hour along the route so I could photograph the snow-covered alps. He never complained about how many breaks we made, no matter where we were. And, despite his protests about how much he hated having his photograph taken, I insisted upon it. In the lead-up to Wayne's sixtieth birthday we hiked for days by the sea-green Galician coast, and then rested at an organic vineyard close to Santiago.

Eventually, we found our way into Portugal, a country my husband had enthused about for months—I'd never understood why. But he was intrigued by both the similarities and the differences between this nation and our adopted Spain: the language they partially shared; the subtle alterations between the flavours and food. We drove across a border that was barely signposted. The air smelled the same as it rushed past our open windows; the country looked the same, too. Until we stopped at a roadhouse and tried to use our Spanish to order lunch. I was told in broken English, politely but directly, please not to use the Spanish. Please to try to use the Portuguese.

Porto was where Wayne turned sixty. Contrary to my expectations, we both adored this harbourside city immediately. There seemed an incongruence between the busy cafes and the peaceful serenity of the golden waterways: it felt somehow more authentic than the grand cities we had seen in Eastern Europe.

The sunshine on the river, a breath of warm air playing on our skin, meant he began to wear cargo shorts and I felt happy to dress in summer skirts. Trams rattled up and down the hillsides across the crowded streets. A framework of iron bridges spanned the channel, beside laneways where washing flapped and wide-eyed children slid down railings to watch the fancy tourists in their fancy restaurants by the wharf. We walked everywhere, all day and half the night. Summer scented the air.

On his birthday, I snuck out of our apartment early. For me, after fifty something years of feeling like a plain Jane, Wayne had given me confidence, and I knew that wearing something sexy for him would afford him enormous pleasure. With a wonderful certainty, I combed the stores.

Mid-morning, on tiptoes, I slipped into the bathroom and undressed in haste. Within the apartment, I could hear that my husband had rolled out of bed and was busily tapping at the keyboard, no doubt checking on routes for our upcoming drive to Lisbon. I knew he had opened the French doors because the sound of the traffic hummed from three floors below.

I stepped into the full light of the day.

'Well, look at you.' He rose from the chair in one movement.

'Happy Birthday,' I said, corny as Marilyn Monroe singing for the President. I had the grace to blush.

A blushing face and sentimental words didn't interest him. With the sun entering the room, filtering through the open doorway, he made love to me.

'I adore you,' I whispered over and over. 'I adore you.'

That night, after some whispered conversations with the owner of the apartments, partly in English, partly Spanish, and a little Portuguese—and after coercing my husband into the suit he'd bought in Madrid—I pushed Wayne into a taxi for 'a magical mystery tour'.

I'd arranged a degustation dinner to celebrate his birthday. The restaurant sat high on the hills on the opposite side of the river. Before our meal, the manager escorted Wayne on a private tour through halls holding barrel after barrel of precious port. We feasted at a table spread with a white linen cloth, surveying the city at dusk.

Later that evening, within the darkness of the city, he unlocked the front door to the apartment building, while I lagged behind, tipping the taxi driver.

'I could hear you laughing with him,' he said to me after I raced across the stones and met him at the entrance, '... you were laughing into the night.'

Then he kissed me. 'Thank you, Suz. I've waited sixty years for someone to care enough about me to give me a birthday celebration like that.'

Our Porto. Built of bookshops and cafes and restless individuals hurrying along the pavement. It was a place of wine bars and couples bickering on the street; doors opening and closing from blinding light to opaque gloom.

16

Sintra, 19 June 2015

WE ARRIVED IN LISBON TWO days after Wayne's birthday. And left the capital the very next morning on a day trip. We were heading into the cooler hilltops of Sintra, an hour away by road along the Atlantic coast.

Looking like a village from a Brothers Grimm fairytale, this legendary town was perched halfway up a mountainside. Around every bend of the road, I glimpsed medieval castles set against dappled sunlight and green gardens. Once the summer residences of European royal families, every palace appeared storybook perfect. Yellow turrets rose from forests of oak and maple, holly and hawthorn. The air was temperate. I imagined the woods concealed deer, possibly magical creatures from another time. But I remember how silent Wayne was. I remember how I slid my eyes away from the view and was immediately drawn by the way his hands clenched and unclenched the steering wheel.

'You all right, sweetheart?'

'Just concentrating.'

I shifted my eyes back to the road. We were searching for the remote Convent of the Capuchos, hidden high in the hills, amongst the forest.

I heard him stifle a sigh.

'Sure you're feeling all right, love?'

And he snapped. 'Just shut up will you, Susan!'

It was like someone had flung me by the wrist into a brick wall. All the breath rushed from me and immediately the tears stung.

He steered the car over onto the gravel. Off the road. The crunch of pebbles rolled under the wheels. He turned off the ignition. Reached for my hand. My face.

'I'm sorry. I'm sorry, sweetheart. I don't know what's wrong with me.'

Nodding blindly, I was unable to meet his eyes—it still felt like I was planted against an imaginary wall. He leant across and kissed my cheek.

'Are you all right?'

I patted his knee awkwardly. 'It's okay.' And I tried to push his behaviour to the back of my mind.

We entered the Franciscan monastery grounds alone. Other than the breeze through the trees, and some tiny jaybirds whistling in the oak trees, the morning was silent. We climbed beyond the forest, up a rise of stone steps and along a path etched with lichen. Visible in the centre of the footpath was a stone cross—about two feet high. Other than the ferns sweeping across the trail, the limestone cross stood alone, a singular presence in shifting shafts of light. We began to whisper.

I ran my fingers across the golden green lichen on an old wooden gate behind the cross. It splintered under my skin.

Swinging it open, we faced a staircase carved into the mountain, and ascended through a tunnel of maple trees. A purple hydrangea signposted the way.

From there we moved into a forest clearing laid with cobble-stones. The space was perhaps five metres square and open to the elements. The rock walls were blanketed with creepers. A giant slab of granite, shaped into a table, was surrounded by a bench made of rock and cushioned in green moss. I glanced ahead, following the path with my eyes. The monks' quarters were all made from the same stone—fashioned in and around trees that had been standing for hundreds of years—the church, the kitchen and the sleeping cells had all been constructed against the cliff face, created from giant, granite boulders.

My husband turned his face to me once, his eyes blazing in the sun. Then he began to wander from one cavern to the next. The incident in the car was forgotten.

'You know this number eight they've carved into the rock walls is meant to represent infinity?' he called out over his shoulder. I nodded, even though he couldn't see me. He was talking to himself as much as to me.

Reading aloud from the guide pamphlet, he said, 'the monks lived a solitary life. They made no attempt to convert other people. They worshipped the earth. Raised plants and herbs and their animals. They lived here, off the land, in these mountains, trying to make as minimal impact on the environment as possible.' I'd never seen him more stirred about the spiritual.

Leading the way, Wayne searched all the secret pathways. He searched all the private, shadowed rooms. He bent to enter a cave; its small, square-cut window cleaved from the very side of the mountain; he straightened up to explore a sun-drenched court-yard. Several times he circled the old tree in the middle of the main square, his eyes drawn by its thick boughs that opened up to the sky.

Held in my heart, now, is this image of my husband as he moves forward. I watch as he walks away from me; so tall, so fine.

17

Lisbon, 23 June 2015

I SIP MY COFFEE IN our rented apartment, four floors above the pastel-painted houses along the street. I'm feeling lazy. Half the morning has already passed. I'm contemplating various ideas about what we should do with the rest of the day. Perhaps ride the trams? Cruise the river? Discover some curious little cafe in a back laneway where we can sit and eat spicy Portuguese food.

Lisbon is sunny. Muggy. Flashes of bright blue sky outside the window. Blue tiles on the houses around us shine in the strong sunlight. The harbour below is vast. The water stretches so far, I can't see where it ends.

And there's a noise—a sound I don't recognise. I think almost . . . is it fear?

My head snaps in the direction of Wayne, who is still asleep in the room beyond. My big bear of a husband is never frightened. But that's the emotion I recognise. Fear stalks the space between us.

Staggering into the stifling room, I discover Wayne arched backwards between the sheets. He is half sitting up; his body crooked into a question mark of agony. My man, propped on one arm, groans.

His face is purple; he suffers. Something is throttling the life from his body. He stares beyond awareness; alone in the fight he is losing.

'Wayne! God!'

I rush forward and stupidly pat his back. Shake my head in confusion at what I'm doing—and then I *run*!

I run to my phone, discarded on the floor in the lounge room. Near the power point. But it's not plugged in—and it's dead. I twist in the room. Slam in the plug. Grab Wayne's phone. But his password? My laptop . . . What's the emergency number? Googling. Scrolling frantically down a page, all written in Portuguese. What number do I ring? I snatch up my phone. Dance from one device to the other. Read the emergency number off the screen. Punch in the sequence. Hear the screech of a flat line. I punch again. Flat line. Scroll up and down the screen. Why can't I get through? The number, the number . . . why isn't this working? I hear silence. Too locked into what I'm attempting to do, I do not glance into the other room. Instead, I run. It's a conscious choice. Don't look, don't look. Keep going. Keep going. You have to keep trying.

Outside and across the hall, I pound on the neighbours' door. Sprint down the hall because they do not answer immediately. Speed backwards. Forwards. Up and down that corridor like a mouse in a maze. What do I do? What do I do? My God, what am I going to do?

'Mi marido mi marido,' I yell into the face of the woman from across the way who has finally opened the door.

'Ambulancia. Ambulancia.' And dreadfully, because I can't find the words, I mime what I think my husband looks like as he is dying. But I am insufficient.

I fly back to the bedroom. Wayne has collapsed face down. To stay? Or to run?

Winding around, I recognise emergency procedures on the back of the door. But it's the same number as the one I've already tried.

I punch it in again. And again. But there's no answer. I shriek to no one. Over and over.

Gradually, a grey window shade releases in my mind. There is a dawning knowledge. I don't want to acknowledge it. I keep trying.

The middle-aged woman from across the way has now understood and tries ringing an alternate number. Flat line for her too. With sharp indications, she hurries her teenage daughter down the four floors to the ground, 'to use fixed phone'.

Then, time begins to slow. How long have I been doing this?

I scurry back towards our apartment, motion the woman to come in. *Please help me?* I will direct her efforts. She can ring for the ambulance again. I will revive my husband.

But she shakes her head. Her eyes reluctant. She will not come in.

I climb onto the bed. Heave Wayne onto his side. He is so heavy yet so pliable. I uncurl the thick tongue from out of his throat with my finger. He makes a long sigh. Then nothing. I spend what seems like hours with two fingers on his throat. Is he dead or am I just not doing it right? I roll him on his back and attempt mouth-to-mouth resuscitation, but I cannot make a seal, his mouth is too wide and too slack. Where is the ambulance?

Spinning back out into the hallway, the mother and daughter are standing still. The girl tells me in her broken English she believes she has contacted the ambulance service. But I hear only my own breathing slamming up against the morning.

I sprint down the four flights of concrete stairs and fly onto the street, a mad woman, barely dressed. I am screaming. The film has speeded up again. Realisation is flooding my heart.

There is a young man, his back to me, wandering down the hill in the sunshine. I grab him with both hands, wail at him about *'mi marido es morte'*. He understands. Presses the buttons to dial the number he knows by heart. I remain beside him on the bright street, eyes peeled, heaving to breathe. Is he truly speaking with emergency services? He looks at me. Makes a face. The address? The street he urges? We both look around wildly for a signpost. But finally, finally I understand, that someone is coming to help me.

And the door? What do I do about the ambulance officers getting into the building? The young stranger offers to wait till they arrive.

I race back up the four flights of stairs. Lurch along the corridor. Snatch a breath.

Then I stop at the door to the apartment. Hold myself straighter. Walk into the bedroom with my fists clenched. I know it's too late. I've taken too long.

Lowering myself on the bed, beside my dead husband, I raise my eyes up to the ceiling and swallow hard, search for some dignity to show him as the tears begin to fall. It seems very important. To show him dignity. I pick up the hand of the man I love and I hold it in mine, stroke his forearm over and over. Sit. Wait. Whisper to him, 'Please Wayne, my darling. Please. I can't bear it.'

18

Lisbon, 23 June 2015

HOURS AND HOURS FOLLOW AND I'm an aimless stranger upon a floating landscape. I feel like I exist on a piece of driftwood in a vast ocean.

This place is flat. Lengths of sand stretch far in one direction and then far the other way. Sometimes I recognise the planeness of cement. I can see a shimmer of heat lying across everything. Like a mirage, the edges of what seems to be a beach grow then recede around me. There is too much space. There are no boundaries keeping me safe. I imagine I will fall off the edge of the world.

Then suddenly the universe collapses. I am going to suffocate.

Bright lights blind me ... in ... and out ... of life ... Light blooms ... light dies.

My skin peels off my bones.

My soul fuses to these strange surroundings.

For hours, the bodies about me are people with whom I'm unfamiliar—who speak a language to me I can't understand. Their mouths open and shut and I can't hear them. I am looking at the rest of the world through a thick pane of glass and nothing seems tangible.

Two sets of paramedics had worked on Wayne. And one doctor. The first team of paramedics dragged Wayne off the bed, and I leapt up to cradle his head so it wouldn't hit the cement floor. They positioned me over Wayne and demonstrated to me that I was to perform CPR while they stuck a tube down his throat to open his airways. Another two paramedics arrived. Then a doctor. Then the police. From an empty room it became crowded. For over forty minutes they all tried. But no signs of life were detected.

Half a day later, Angela from the Australian embassy shuffles all the strangers out of the apartment. Ushers me down the stairs.

'You need to come outside with me. You don't want to see this.'

We wait up the hill, our eyes averted, while attendants transfer Wayne into the back of a hearse. I trail my husband's body to the morgue—in a taxi barrelling along Lisbon's crowded streets. The unguarded noises of summer stab at me through the windows. But there is more than one morgue and I have somehow directed the driver to the wrong one.

Later, much later, afternoon sunshine crashes upon me unexpectedly through the skylight when I return to the apartment. The hotel owner has repeatedly assured me he is happy to shift me to another room but I violently shake my head. I must remain close to Wayne.

The maids have been. There is the maw of an empty, freshly made bed—sanitised, smoothed and straightened. How did they get the wee out, I wonder?

That first night, I lie on the bed. The bed in which Wayne had died twelve hours earlier. I lie still and stare out the window at the moon. If I stay motionless, this dreadful, incomprehensible thing will stay away from me. I am desperately afraid of falling apart.

Below the window, the city is hidden, but black sky and the endless harbour fill the aluminium frame. Logically, I realise that a massive shift has occurred in my world. Like a slab of earth has been cleaved off. I'm also aware that this event is soon going to split my life apart, but my heart has not yet caught up with my head. Gazing at the moon, it is impossible for me to accept the magnitude of Wayne's death, so I lie like a stiff little girl, imagining Wayne looking down on me. I stay awake till dawn—unmoving between the sheets, staring at the moon, waiting for a sign from Wayne that never comes.

Two disembodied days of unintelligible *policia* interviews follow. Dry-eyed, I sign statements that I do not understand.

Then Jonno disembarks, from the first available plane he was able to catch from Sydney. We hunch in the back seat of the hearse; people cross themselves on the streets at the sight of us and the action forces me to physically experience a more ancient respect for death. I glance behind me to the bulk of the extra-broad coffin the funeral home has ordered in. A cloth of rich purple velvet lies draped across the gleaming wood, plush in the morning sun. It is extraordinarily beautiful.

The crematorium is a concrete building set amongst the hills surrounding Lisbon. Jonno and I sit at the front of the chapel, alone on a pew. Behind us, lined up like a file of silent soldiers, are row after row of empty seats.

'Who will witness the coffin entering the furnace?'

'I will,' my son says.

And gently. 'It's okay for you to cry, Mum.'

19

Granada, July 2015

WEEKS LATER, JONNO STEERED US back through the empty desert of the Portuguese countryside, through Southern Spain and into Granada— with me, tightly buckled in beside him—in the hire car. We carried Wayne's ashes on the back seat, halfway across two countries.

Somewhere, on that dreadful morning, between the doctor pronouncing Wayne dead as he lay like he'd been crucified on the cement floor of the apartment, and when Angela, the represent- ative from the Australian embassy arrived, I thought to ring my son. He'd been the one to notify foreign affairs in Australia, who'd immediately sent Angela. Angela, my angel. She argued with the police about moving the body sooner rather than later to the morgue. She explained the legal processes and all the certificates and translations of these certificates that I would need. She arranged with the owners of the building to let me extend my stay, while a seemingly endless series of physical and bureaucratic procedures were undertaken. She fussed about me eating. Suggested I have a shower. She connected me with the funeral home that organised the cremation.

'We need your marriage certificate,' Rosa from the funeral home said as she sat across from me, a week after Wayne's death. 'That you are his next of kin needs to be established or otherwise we can't release his body to you. We can't allow you to cremate his body.'

By some miracle, I'd brought most of our documentation with us on the trip to Portugal. We'd reasoned it was safer than leaving the precious forms of identity in Granada. I offered up Wayne's birth certificate, along with the marriage certificate for Rosa to inspect. Relinquished his passport with trembling fingers to Angela, who was also there. It felt so final. To give up Wayne's passport. What if he needed it later?

But when Rosa asked for a suit in which to dress Wayne, no shoes required, Jonno had to help me up, help me stumble across to the suitcase.

'You're okay, Mum. I'm here.'

Jonno had also, on that morning, thought to ring my brother, Pete. And he rang Di, and Liz's husband, Geoff. Who shared the news with Caitlin and Ashleigh. Jonno later told me both Di and Geoff had been on standby to fly to Portugal.

I couldn't tell Wayne's mother, Martha. Instead, like a coward, I rang one of Wayne's brothers who lived in Brisbane and asked him to contact Martha. In the following days, I also spoke to some of Wayne's friends and rang my former colleagues at the school where I taught. The conversation I most regret was a phone call I made to a great mate of Wayne's who was collecting his mail while we were away. Mistakenly, I believed this man also knew Wayne's best friend Darren—who I couldn't reach at the time because he was working. Subsequently, at my request, Allison, Darren's wife—who had known Wayne for more than twenty years because both men had worked in the same mines—received a phone call from a total stranger informing her of the shocking news.

Mobile phone connections had been near impossible, however. Unreliable, intermittent at best. If I remember correctly, using the phone on Messenger was the only way I could contact anyone, whereas people from Australia seemed better able to reach me. Part of the reason I'd been so afraid to call Martha was because I imagined informing her of her son's death and a terrible, 'What? What?' repeating down the unpredictable phone connection. Back in Granada, the phones worked better, which was a relief, because seven days later Jonno left Spain to return to Australia. He was needed back at work.

I remained behind for another few weeks, throwing out or giving away the possessions Wayne and I had collected over the last six months: books, an expensive computer chair he'd bought, the wine we'd carted all the way from Prague. How could I possibly carry these things home?

I also needed to say goodbye to people. Our tutors from Spanish school. Our former classmates. Friends we'd made. There were places I wanted to visit in the city one last time. I wasn't ready to leave our dreams behind quite yet. So, I held the worst of my grief at bay. Because I knew, even then, that once I left Spain, Wayne would finally cease to exist. Who would remember this place and us in it, and all the wonder we'd experienced, once I went home? Crammed into three rooms, living together every hour, we'd shared a lengthened moment in time. The walks we loved, the food we loved, the places we loved—they would remain something only we could ever appreciate. They existed in a context no one else could grasp.

But cleaving Wayne and me in two did not seem sufficient retribution to satisfy the gods. The happiness we'd shared had a price, one I was beginning to discover I must keep paying.

It was high summer in Granada, and tourists overran the streets. There was no space to breathe in the unbearable heat. I trekked up the Al Sabikah hill one last time, wandered above the Alhambra to my favourite spot, amongst fields of olive trees with a view of the Sierra Nevada range in the distance. There was a vantage point where I could see the city. But suddenly, as I stared down at the places we'd loved, my nose started to bleed. It wouldn't stop. And I had left Wayne's big square of a cotton handkerchief in my other bag. I didn't even have a tissue. When I tried to twist my shirt up it was too short to reach my face. It was a bizarre and unexpected experience.

Every time I tilted my head back, walking across the hillside, I prayed it would make the blood stop running. I was so desperate that I searched for anything on the ground, leaves or grass, but the hillside was bare and brown. I was forced to enter the only building I knew—back down the hill—an impressive hotel. In front of a crowd of tourists eating their lunch, hands slicked with my own blood, my face smeared, I begged for help. This seemed a needless addition to my wretchedness. Had I not paid enough already?

Yet, still, the gods were dissatisfied. In Portugal, we'd begun to run out of cash. Wayne had been considering accessing part of his super-annuation for us to use as funds, to live on for the remainder of the year. So now, money was short and my worries were long. I'd paid for the cremation in Lisbon. I had no idea how much Wayne's memorial service would cost back in Orange. Or what my living expenses would be. Or even where I would live. With no easy access to funds to pay for excess baggage—I was now deemed a single traveller, my baggage allowance cut in half—I could not afford to take what I wanted home with me. I was forced to throw out most of his clothes.

In between phone calls to Di, where I sobbed so much I can't remember if I even said a single word, and a gasping, disconnected conversation with Martha, were tortured discussions with travel agents and the insurance company back home. We'd purchased standard insurance, had waived extra cover for physical activities like riding motorbikes or skiing.

'No way,' Wayne had laughed, 'we're going on an adventure, but we're not that crazy!'

The insurance company explained to me that the tickets I'd already paid for, the ones for our planned return journey home next January, would not be refunded or exchanged, 'at this point in time'. I was obliged to purchase a new ticket. Lovely Jaimie, Jonno's girlfriend at the time, was the one who made a fuss on social media and forced the insurance company to act more compassion-ately. At the beginning of August, after I returned to Australia, I received a reimbursement for the cremation costs and a refund on Jonno's ticket—for some reason that was seen as a cost that required compensation.

But in Spain, with no knowledge of what the future might bring, I was hoarding whatever money was left and worrying.

Most of my summer clothes I had to shove into the same garbage skip as my husband's shirts. I would need my winter clothes once I was back in Australia—my life was turning into a game of survival.

I kept Wayne's old leather jacket, his RM Williams boots, the cologne I'd bought him in Dubai on the way over, some of his flannelette shirts and his reading glasses—but nothing else. Because there were the ashes. Ten extra kilos that had to be factored into my luggage allowance. He was, as Rosa from the funeral home had stated with a frown, a big man. I'd never considered that the larger a person is, the more ash there would be.

At the end of July, I finally began my journey home. Turned the key on the front door of our apartment for the last time. The container of ashes rested in the bottom of the computer bag, hung over my left shoulder. With each hand, I dragged my two remaining suitcases behind me—through the city, across the cobblestones, to the Granada train station.

There, I hauled myself onto a connecting bus to travel to the Antequera train station—due to track work. An hour later, I fell off the connecting bus at Antequera, and stumbled through the security turnstiles, explaining in broken Spanish what I carried in the computer bag. Tears coursed down my face.

I heaved the two suitcases onto a train where people sat atop each other, such were the summer crowds, and then manoeuvred myself and the luggage off the train at Madrid, three hours later— the crowds eventually pushing me from behind because I did not have the physical strength left to drag both bags at the same time.

Up the escalator at the Madrid Estacion de Atocha, and the lip of one suitcase caught in the teeth of the escalator. Then the computer bag slid off my shoulder as the snagged suitcase dragged me sideways. The heat and tears continued to dribble down my face.

I was exhausted. The bags were too heavy. As I sprawled in the back seat of a taxi speeding to the airport (my one concession) I calculated quantities. I figured I weighed 65 kilos and the combined weight of two suitcases, the computer bag and my handbag weighed about the same. It had been days since I'd slept. I couldn't stop worrying that I was still carrying too much weight for the flight, but I had nothing more I could throw away.

Weeping still, I checked in at the Emirates desk at the airport. Every time I tried to speak, the tears began afresh. And, there, this seemingly endless journey home began to illustrate the significance of strangers in times of tragedy. I never discovered the cost of my excess baggage because the woman from Emirates led me into an office to sit quietly, away from the curious eyes of other passengers. And even though I was flying economy, she escorted me to the first-class lounge where I was allowed to rest till the flight boarded. There was no upgrade on the plane, but she'd kindly allocated me a row of three seats, all by myself. There was a four-hour layover in Dubai. I was dreading it. And it turned out I had cause to be anxious.

Carrying a person's ashes from one country to another, on board a plane, is a complicated procedure. It is more significant these days, the police in Lisbon explained, due to the heightened risk of terrorists and what may be concealed in carry-on luggage.

Three police officers, a funeral home representative and Angela from the Consulate, along with Jonno and I, had all stood in the apartment one morning, in early July, while elaborate efforts were made to parcel up Wayne's ashes. One uniformed man jammed the ashes into a steel canister and secured it with an official wax seal to prove the police had witnessed what material went into the canister and that they were present when it was sealed. Then I scrawled my signature under that of the *Comanda Metropolitano de Lisboa,* to certify I was transporting ashes from Granada, through Madrid, through Dubai, to Sydney. Additionally, all the paperwork, officiated by the Portuguese authorities, needed to document, ahead of time, the exact route I would take, and each means of transport for my journey from one country to the next: the train from Granada to Madrid, the plane from Madrid to Dubai, the plane from Dubai to Sydney. Each of the dates and identification of flight numbers had to be noted as well. The Secretary at the Australian Consulate translated this document, as well as the death register record and the cremation certificate, and also attached the *Apostille*, to certify the 'capacity of the signer and the seal'.

But I worried that the margin for what could go wrong was both too narrow and too wide. What would happen, for example, if flight numbers changed or a flight was delayed? What would happen, if for some reason I lost the paperwork or missed a connection? I was desperate not to break the chain that was allowing me to take my husband home.

But something did go wrong.

In spite of the Portuguese *policia*, the Australian embassy and the funeral home in Lisbon all assuring me the paperwork was in order, the airport official at Dubai, in his official navy-blue uniform, was having none of it.

Hundreds of travellers milled about like cattle in the security hall. The noise was so loud it hung heavy as a tarpaulin above our heads. Lines of hot, tired tourists stretched behind me; a nightmare lit in harsh fluorescence.

I was shaking. The guard indicated to me sharply, again and again, to put the canister carrying the ashes through the X-ray machine.

'I have to explain . . .' I faltered. But I laid the canister on the conveyer belt anyway.

'It's ashes,' I said, as the official behind the computer screen gestured to the guard, spoke to him in exclamations.

'Again,' he ordered.

'Excuse me,' I said to the American guy behind me, and I stumbled back to where the conveyer belt started.

The other guards trod closer, intrigued. They argued. Peered at me. Pointed at the X-ray screen.

The guard shook his head

'Again,' pointing to the back of the line.

Shaking my head, I refused to move, flapped about with the paperwork, trying to find the English translation from the Portuguese embassy. Scattered the pages across the counter.

The guard shouted something at me but I couldn't understand him. A uniformed woman standing beside him started to giggle.

As I became more frantic, I stabbed with my fingers at the documentation laid out on the black rubber mat. And I watched the woman whisper to the guard, flirting with him, apparently amused by my emerging panic. He was distracted by her like a fly buzzing in his ear.

And the crowd were getting restless behind me.

'What's the hold up?' an American voice shouted.

'Undo it,' the guard barked, pointing at the container I was holding.

Undo the canister holding the dust and bones of my darling husband?

I shook my head. 'I can't.'

This infuriated him.

But all I could think about was how would I ever get Wayne home? The lid of the canister had to be fixed tight—and the package needed to remain whole, like the papers stated. Nothing was to be disturbed.

Finally, the guard examined my forms.

'You have a letter, yes, from Portuguese police. But this letter is not from Dubai police. You must get documentation here in Dubai. You cannot go through.'

Then I fell apart, started screaming at him—and everything went dead quiet, and I was forgetting to care about being respectful, like Jonno had instructed; forgetting to care about not making a scene. I remember gesticulating wildly, stamping my feet, shrieking at the man.

He stepped back.

'This,' I sneered, and thrust the cylinder forward, 'is my *husband*! What am I supposed to do if you don't let me through? Where will I go?'

I could hear people shouting behind me. I felt warm bodies pressing up against me. Then the security guard wrestled the ashes away from me.

And I was begging that arsehole, with the gun at his hip, and the mean, cloudy attitude. 'If you don't let me through, I will never get us home. Don't you understand?' I was yelling at him with my arms crossed over my head, walking in circles. 'You can't open it,' and I snatched the canister back from him. 'Once you tear that seal open it can never be repaired. We'll be stuck here forever.'

Hours later, I peered out the small window to the earth below. The guard had given up mostly, I believe, because the American men behind me made a fuss about the hold-up. I was let off with a warning.

'Next time make sure you have the correct papers.'

So, there I was—suspended in flight, suspended between the old and the new, between my life with my husband and my life without him, suspended between two hemispheres, suspended between two worlds, suspended between space and earth, suspended between night and day. The passengers around me were asleep. A golden city was below us, lit like a lantern in the desert. I had no idea where we were.

'Cairo,' said the pretty young air stewardess, and she slipped into the empty seat beside me and made me cry again, such was her concern. She comforted me for a moment. But her comfort was a false harbour. Because then she told me about her grandfather who had recently died, gave me a hug and promised me, 'God makes all things happen for a reason. God always has a plan.'

And I remembered Wayne's words from the day we'd sat in the sun, so excited about leaving Australia. *There is no evidence of a benevolent god.* Thousands of miles above the earth, I was felled by the truest and most bitter realisation of my life: There is no evidence of a benevolent God and I am utterly alone.

As we neared Sydney, the lights blinked on in the cabin, the sickly smell of scrambled eggs swelled alongside my anxiety, and I nearly gagged. All the explanations I was anticipating giving, the weight of luggage I wasn't sure I could carry one step further, caused me to clench my fingers round the plastic handle of the canister I had insisted remain in my lap. My greatest fear was that having made it home, some minor technicality, right at the end of this horror, would deny me entry into Australia.

However, the stuttered explanation I tried to give to the female customs officer in the declaration hall was redundant.

In a relaxed drawl, she simply said, 'I think you've been through enough already, love. You don't need to show me any of your paper-work. Don't worry about any of that now. And welcome to Sydney.'

Then I walked us through the gates. I walked us home.

20

Country New South Wales, August 2015

IN THE DAYS BEFORE THE service, in the dead of winter, Martha and I barricaded ourselves in the office in her farmhouse, situated a few kilometres outside Orange, with the blow heater switched to high.

From the first moment Wayne had brought me to meet her, we'd connected—through a shared temperament, shared politics and shared interests. We loved reading the same books, we both enjoyed amateur photography and watching English crime shows. I admired the renovations she'd completed at the old farmhouse. And, of course, we loved our dogs. Ours was an immediate and comfortable rapport. I think that even if we had not had Wayne in common, we might have been friends.

In the study that week, I remember us spending hours scrolling through photographs of Wayne. We were arranging albums for the wake. Martha wanted a pictorial record of Wayne's life for people to look through as they stood around chatting and drinking after the service. We cropped, edited and printed images from Europe, keeping ourselves busy, always respectful about each other's grief: alert to each other's requirements. I think that being aware of the

118

other kept some of the more intense grief in check. I repeatedly assured her how happy Wayne had been in Granada in an attempt to provide some comfort. She repeatedly assured me how much Wayne had loved me in an attempt to comfort me. It was a brief safe haven for both of us before the storm.

We debated about which images to use from Spain, which were the most interesting pictures from my husband's childhood in New Guinea. Martha even discovered a few rare photographs of Wayne, snapped in Mt Isa, after he'd finally escaped Goroka in his mid-twenties.

Seeing the photographs from Mt Isa profoundly affected me. The expression of misery and bitterness my husband wore was new to me. This was a man I'd never known—the downcast mouth, the scowling black eyes, an accusatory face, always half-turned away from the lens.

A bittersweet realisation occurred to me while his mother and I worked in that little room together. As my fingers traced over the curled-up polaroids, straightening out damage wreaked by the years—I believed, I really believed, that I finally understood the mystery that was my husband.

'All those words of endearment, the way he would tell me I'd shown him a happiness he'd never known before—they were more truthful than I realised, Martha.'

She nodded. Head down, fingers gripping the scissors, not meeting my eyes.

'In a perverse way, I wish I'd seen these old images before he died.'

Her drawn face lifted to mine. 'Why, sweetheart?'

'I always loved him, cared for him, tried to make him happy. You know that. Yet if I'd had the measure of his unhappiness before we'd met, I would've tried even harder.' I started to sob.

I cannot imagine the despair that Martha felt. I didn't dare try to imagine it. Jonno was so precious to me and I didn't know how she could bear it. Because I knew the way I loved Jonno was the way she felt about Wayne. He was the man she relied on. The son who would take her out to dinner and drive her and her friends on trips around New South Wales. She was the woman from whom the small, innocent boy had been stolen. But somehow, united in different kinds of grief for the same man, we were a solace for each other.

During those hours, those days, when I would snatch an image from the pile and show it to Martha because I had something to explain about where we were in Spain and how Wayne had reacted. Or she would lean against my arm to ask my opinion about what place to crop a picture, something I'd never understood revealed itself: Wayne's belief that I was beautiful finally made sense to me.

Oh, I trusted he'd felt it. I just could never comprehend what he saw, or how he perceived me as lovely. How could he be looking at the same person I saw in the mirror and complimenting me the way he always did? Now, perhaps, those last words he'd whispered to me, at our final meal in the restaurant in Lisbon, the one he'd arranged in such a casual manner during a final text to me—*why don't I come home and take my girl out to some place special?*—were believable.

We'd been seated at a table for two, on the mezzanine level of a traditional Portuguese restaurant. The room was lit in soft pink because the walls were draped in swathes of rose silk and the low lamps reflected the colour off the walls. I remember the dessert was sweet, creamy Portuguese tarts and while we both sipped local sherry he said to me, his hand reaching across to take mine, 'You look beautiful tonight, Suz.'

He'd been abused as a child. Previous relationships had turned sour. My love—this was why I was beautiful to him.

He so often linked the beauty he saw with my 'belonging' to him—my being 'his'. What he meant was that I loved him unconditionally. And for me, who had doubted my physical appearance my whole life, and always felt like I belonged nowhere and belonged to no one, I happily accepted the connection I thought he was making. But now I realised I'd misunderstood. Wayne was seeing the beauty of who I was as a person, because I loved him no matter what. He'd been searching as hard as I had been for a sense of belonging, and he'd found that with me. That was the sorrow that cut my heart.

The morning of the memorial service was freezing. Orange was empty, the roads abandoned. The trees were leafless and the chill of winter buried all sound. In the bottom of my purse, the eulogy I'd written lay beside my husband's handkerchief.

Parking Wayne's ute outside the funeral home, I was astonished by the mass of people. The men! There were men standing about on the pavement, on the street, at the entrance to the chapel. I stared through the window at a group of about twenty of Wayne's loyal crew from the local mine. I stared at men—who later came up to me at the wake—from mines in Kalgoorlie and Mt Isa. Men had flown in from mines all over Australia, from all the places my husband had worked in the past thirty-five years. I stared at these blokes unravelling onto the roadway in small dark knots of uncomfortable suits and ties. Then I cried in the car—before I even climbed out, before the service had even begun—at their conspicuous respect.

Wayne's nephew, Silas, spoke first. This was John's son—the son of Wayne's brother who still lived in New Guinea.

'I'm just so happy my uncle didn't die in the dark, down a mine shaft, thousands of metres under the earth, digging up someone else's gold. He died having the best time of his life, on an amazing adventure, with the woman he loved by his side.'

Then Wayne's best friend stood up. But overcome with grief, Darren couldn't finish what he had to say.

When it was my turn to speak, I shook so badly I could barely turn the first page of the eulogy. So, I forced myself to think of my husband. I used his strength and his pride in me, to straighten up behind the lectern, to take my time and look out over the crowd of people who had come to farewell him. My sense of duty gave me the fortitude to read aloud the words I had so painstakingly written.

'Good morning, and thank you all for coming.

'When I was much younger, and still in school, I read some of my first Shakespeare. It was Antony and Cleopatra. And Shakespeare's words inspired in me the image of a giant of a man. I daydreamed about that man.

'But I honestly never believed such a man still existed in this modern day, or that such a man could ever fall in love with me.

'Then I met this man, this exact man described by Shakespeare. A brave, trustworthy, moral man who owned a compassionate heart, an iron resolution and an enormous capacity to love. A man who exemplified integrity. A man who demonstrated a palpable generosity of spirit.

'And I think then, we simply stirred up the stars too much.

His legs bestrid the ocean,
His rear'd arm crested the world.
His voice was propertied to friends
But when he meant to quail and shake the orbs
He was as rattling as thunder . . .

'Wayne always had me tucked up under his enormous arm, sheltered by his giant shoulders. I was adored. I was safe. I was loved.

'An entire world to me, he was. He steered me straight north.

'While to him—I was his girl, his lover, his wife, his partner.

'And every day he used that extensive vocabulary of his to declare his love for me. This, he would state, my girl, is going to be the best decade of our lives.

'So, some nights this grief, much too hard, threatens to rip my throat apart. What I would steal, borrow, beg to hear again his stories, his observations, his declarations of love—to feel both his arms locked about me.

'Instead, I now need to trust my husband. Believe it will work out. Trust in him still, to look after me.'

Then I faltered. The pages wouldn't separate. I stared at my fingers.

'Jonno?'

My son leapt onto the stage. And the floorboards shook beneath us. He stood beside me at the microphone, my eyes spilling with tears, as the loss swallowed me up.

Before going to sit for lunch at Wayne's favourite pub, I collapsed on the stairs. Someone I didn't know had cornered me at the end of the aisle in the chapel, 'How strong you are, Susan.'

But of course, I wasn't. I was insensible and I don't know how I didn't crumple to the floor. Instead, I tugged up my knees, buried my face and rocked—I cried so hard I thought my body would split open. I'd never wept so desperately in my life. I gave in hopelessly and my desolation took root. A final, bleak space ripped open in front of me and I simply slid in. Even Di could not comfort me, her arms patted my shoulders, my back, but I no longer dwelled within myself. Violent sobs erased me.

❀

A week later, down on the farm, I rested my elbows on Martha's wide veranda railing and wondered in a disconnected way about the point of my life, because the only bloom I could imagine in my future was absence.

Walking the tracks through paddocks of lucerne, trailing along the highways for hours on the pretext of walking Millie, I acted my part in a black-and-white world. I thought, if Wayne met me on the gravel on the side of one of these country highways, he wouldn't recognise me.

It was a sadness without boundaries. Once, I was a woman standing in the Spanish sunlight with a smile just for him, now I was a discarded paper bag tumbling along the roadside, sexless, anonymous, empty. My sense of self had vanished once again. I was afraid everything else had vanished too. The world had been ripped away from me except, somehow, I'd been left behind—in this strange place—where everything was unknown. As the cars flashed by, Wayne let go of my hand for the last time and I was lost. Without him holding my hand I didn't exist.

Complicating things further, I still didn't know what had killed Wayne. I tried to explain to Martha over dinner that night.

'The privacy laws over there mean authorities don't state a cause of death on the death register. Both Wayne's autopsy report and the death certificate won't be released until the extra toxicology testing is completed. We won't know until then. I'm so sorry, Martha.'

Martha's partner, Jack, who was from the Czech Republic—an energetic, wiry man and an enthusiastic home chef—tried explaining it to Martha as well.

'Although Suz has cremated Wayne, and she has the certificate to prove it, why he died will remain a mystery. This is what the staff from the Australian embassy in Lisbon have pronounced. Yes?' He glanced to me for confirmation.

I swallowed a mouthful of red.

'They're all very kind. But they informed me in the clearest terms over the phone yesterday, that given the high level of bureaucracy in Portugal, I could wait up to a year to receive the paperwork. That means it might be a year till we have answers.'

Martha picked up her knife and fork. Neatly cut the meat up on her plate. Absently passed a piece of the lamb Jack had cooked so carefully down to Millie, who was curled across her feet on the floor.

We ate in silence.

Then Jack brought out with a flourish the baked custard he'd spent some time preparing. Tactfully, Martha and I ate. Tried to make conversation. But questions about Wayne's death wouldn't leave me alone. I guess I was seeking reassurance.

'I saw Howard at the funeral home today,' I said. 'He was collecting the banner the guys at the mine made for the service. He tried making a joke with me.'

Jack looked up.

'He said it was clever of me to use a foreign country as the means to divert attention from murdering my husband for his money.'

Jack sat up furiously. Dropped his bread knife so it clattered on the plate.

'Jack, it's okay. I'm here in Australia now, safe and sound. But when I think back to Lisbon, those five or so hours I sat on the bed beside Wayne after he died—yes, there was a police guard posted in the next room. Another officer even swapped places with the first one, because the authorities couldn't decide whether to give permission for Wayne's body to be moved.'

Martha continued to play with her dessert but Jack responded.

'You think you were under suspicion?'

'Maybe . . .'

'And another thing,' I continued. 'Wayne's mechanic bailed me up at the wake and asked me if I'd thought about Wayne having undiagnosed epilepsy.' I looked across at Martha. 'Did he ever suffer from epilepsy, Martha?'

She swallowed the tiniest spoonful of baked custard. 'No, darling.'

'The mechanic claimed people die from undiagnosed epilepsy all the time, and that if I'd removed his tongue from his throat earlier, he may have lived.'

Jack pooh-poohed the idea with some Czech words I didn't understand, but such ideas came close to sending me crazy. My guilt about not having been able to save Wayne needled my insides. Sometimes it was hard to breathe, walk or talk. The notion that I may not have cleared his airways soon enough caused my insides to fracture apart—all those millions of bits and pieces under my skin, tethered together so tenuously. I felt that without my covering of flesh, I would have shattered apart, exploded across the earth.

And I remembered my husband, who rarely criticised me, saying days before his death, somewhat snappishly, 'You are the most impractical woman I've ever met.' Had my panic been the thing that killed him? If I'd been more level-headed would he still be alive?

Also, there was no money.

'Martha, I'm afraid I need to leave. My brother, Pete, has offered me a bedroom at his place near Newcastle, and until I get a job, or some money is released from the estate, I need to accept his offer. I can't afford to stay here anymore.'

So, I moved again, to Lake Macquarie, where I filled pointless days cooking meals for my nieces, using recipes I'd learnt in Spain. I shopped for sweet paprika at Coles and attempted not to be a burden, because that's what adopted children do. And that's what some grief-stricken people do, too. I functioned on autopilot. I was still defending myself against a loss that was too great to bear. I scoured job sites on the computer, applying meticulously for work I never intended to try. I washed my remaining clothes. I stacked dishes. No one suggested I act so stoically or expected any meals to be cooked. But my drive to be busy and remain in control kept moving me forwards.

Privacy was what I craved, though. I dreamed of sitting in some silent room, gazing at my husband's photograph. Fantasised about smoothing my hand along the soft leather of his old jacket and ordering his books along a wall.

Then, a small amount of travel insurance was reimbursed to me, and I immediately rented a tiny, two-bedroom cottage, forty-five minutes north of Lake Macquarie, in the rural village of Morpeth. I spent one-fifth of this money on bond and rent in advance.

Jan, my sister-in-law, took me shopping at Kotara before I moved.

'Suz, you need to buy this,' she pointed to a doona with a red sale sticker, 'as well as those blue coffee mugs, and we'll go next door for the essentials—cutlery, a kettle and a can opener. Some teaspoons too.' I trailed after her like a child. She also packed me a care box, with salt, coffee, sugar.

On a coolish Saturday morning, my brother and my son loaded up Wayne's ute with Mum's old furniture, some spare blankets, two bath towels, and I moved—squabbling ungraciously with Pete about which way I wanted the coffee table to face—and Millie, still imagining she was living on Martha's farm, christened the ugly carpet with a wee. For three months, I washed everything by hand because I couldn't afford a washing machine. A friend of Jan's lent me the fridge from their garage.

But all I wanted was my husband. I wanted him to watch with pride as I somehow screwed together the flat-pack bookcase—bought because it was the cheapest I could find—because I had no furniture. We sold it all, remember, Wayne? I wanted him to still be here so he could be proud of my strength. I wanted to talk to him. I wanted him to hold me tight in his arms. I wanted to point out to him that there on ABC news was the train station in Budapest where we'd stood together four months ago. And now see, Wayne? It is overrun by desperate refugees cramming onto trains going nowhere. This is the Europe we just walked through. There is the platform we lingered on. Look at what is happening in the world! The largest wave of refugees the world has ever seen. These wretched people are searching for a place to call home. And me, I'm searching for my place, again, this time without you.

I began to dissolve completely.

Wayne 'saw' me. In this world, he gave me a sense of place and he understood me. He saw the beauty in me. Because of his love I *existed*. He saw my flabby belly. He saw me sick. He brushed my hair. He kissed my lips. He dragged me to the dentist. He undressed me when I was drunk on gin in Granada. He held me close to him with his great arms. He knew me completely and therefore I was.

I lay in bed at night and replayed over and over the first night we'd spent in Granada. The snow was falling softly from the blackest sky I'd ever seen. We were spooning in our narrow bed. He'd pulled me in close and whispered, 'Meeting you has been like getting a second chance at life ... actually, more like getting a second chance at living. Living ... that is the distinction! I'm just so glad I cartwheeled your way, Suz. You have made my life!'

But his death, at this point, had unmade mine. I felt less than I'd been before I met him. Less than I'd been before I'd started searching for Enid and O'Connor. Less than before Liz had died.

21

Morpeth, September 2015

FOR MY BEST FRIEND DI, the relocation she'd desperately wanted for years, from Sydney back to Newcastle, had meant accepting short-term contract work till a full-time job eventuated. She'd shifted back home and bought a sunlit house by the lake in the month Wayne and I moved to Granada. Now, by the most wonderful twist of fate, she worked in communications close to Morpeth. So, almost every afternoon, on her 45-minute drive home, she dropped in for coffee with me, or simply for a walk. My friend might be pretty, fragile-looking, at times the most self-deprecating woman in the world, but she was also bloody stubborn and loyal beyond anything I believed I was worthy of.

One afternoon, we strolled by the swollen Hunter River under a line of willow trees, their leaves trailing through the water.

'Nobody tells you anything about the grief a widow suffers, Di. Nobody warns you.'

She linked her fingers through mine.

'How many times did we talk about what we expected childbirth was going to be like? Or marriage? Remember all those long discussions about flowers and dresses and music?' I paused, and we both stopped, gazing across the river to the floodplains.

'Those long telephone conversations we had about Liz? Why she died? How she died.'

'What are you trying to say, Suz?'

I looked up at the sky, searching for my words.

'You expect a wedding, you expect a child, and so it's part of the conversation you have with friends, because it's part of the expected fabric of your life. Even the death of your parents is an accepted dialogue to have over coffee. God. How often have we talked about Mum? And what's going to happen to her when the time comes?'

Di turned away from the river, turned to me.

'So, isn't it reasonable to consider, once you fall in love, that you might at some point think about which one of you is going to die first?'

We ventured a little further, but someone had erected a barbed-wire fence. Hunched against the wind, we shuffled back to the cottage.

'Becoming a widow happens to other women. I always imagined they didn't care anymore, or had their emotions under control. It was never made real to me. Nobody tells you, Di.' I was crying again. She helped me up the stairs into the house.

In the little kitchenette Di made coffee for us both. Remarked on the black-and-white photograph of Wayne and me, propped against the lounge room wall.

Sighing, I said, 'I spent a lot of money I didn't have getting it printed and framed.'

'Tell me, muchacho,' she encouraged me. 'Where was it taken? Why's it so special to you?'

'It's Javea.' I stood up, laid the coffee mug on the table and lifted up the photograph. 'Javea is a secluded village by the Mediterranean

Sea. We stayed there for a few nights when we came home from the Czech Republic. Despite all the overdevelopment along that part of the Spanish seaboard, the actual town is pretty much in its original state. Beer was cheap. The *pulpo* was the freshest we ever tasted because it was delivered daily, straight from the boats chugging out to sea each dawn.'

With a smile Di asked, 'And is there a reason why you're standing on a wall?'

Staring down at the photograph I explained how Wayne had lifted me up on the sea wall for a bit of a laugh. To make us look like we were the same size.

'If anything, it emphasises the height difference between you,' Di said.

I swallowed. Wayne looked tall; he looked ready to catch me. There was an imagined sense of movement in this image. Scrutinising it, I could almost anticipate jumping into his arms.

'Even though it cost so much, I wanted this particular image printed because of the intimacy it shows. How comfortable we look together. His right arm wrapped about my knees. My hip nestled, curved, into the side of his chest.'

Di nodded.

'And see how we are turned inwards, slightly towards each other? Every part of our self that could touch the other does. We were one body with two heads, four arms and four legs.'

Ironically, or perhaps fearfully, I felt I had been tainted by the original tale I'd told him, the one by Aristophanes. Would being separated from Wayne mean that for the rest of my life I would have to search for that 'wholeness' I'd had with him? Was I always going to remain incomplete?

We'd celebrated this myth. It explained to both him and to me the magnitude of what we meant to each other. Equally, in death, my fragmented perception of self made dreadful sense. I began to despair. How could I survive in such a fractured state? With half of me missing?

After Di left, I sat alone in my tiny house in Morpeth and wept. I ached for my husband—his shoulders, his hard chest, his vast forearms—the satisfaction and sense of completeness when he entered me. I lusted after my dead husband. I was still hopelessly in love with him.

22

Morpeth, September 2015

IT HAD BEEN TEN WEEKS since the memorial service and, in those days, I was still crying every time someone spoke to me. I remember one particular day at the supermarket, at Green Hills. An elderly lady had defended me when a young woman, mobile phone jammed against her ear, red laptop case swinging off her shoulder, barged in front of me in the line at the checkout.

'This woman was here first,' the older woman hissed, indicating me, dressed in baggy tracksuit pants and one of Wayne's oversized flannelette shirts. Trying to thank her for representing me proved impossible. I was sobbing before I even looked in her direction. I couldn't bear the present. I couldn't see the future. I didn't want a future. I just wanted Wayne back and for things to be the way they were. I wanted to be with him so badly that dying seemed a preferable option to life.

That week, my son came up from Sydney for the day, ostensibly to show me his new car. But I knew he was checking on me. I was lost; he understood this. We sat opposite each other on bench seats in the Hog's Breath Cafe in East Maitland. The walls were painted in primary colours. He was ploughing through some kind of double-decker steak while I loaded up with all kinds of carbo-hydrates—chips, battered fish and cheesy garlic bread.

'Mum, what do you imagine it's like for me, being a police officer?'

I shook my head, raised my palms upward in a show of 'I have no idea'.

'Sometimes it feels like there are two worlds.'

My attention focused on my son. For all his boyish good looks, the energy and enthusiasm with which he played sport, the laugh-ter and antics I'd seen in Snapchat images from weekends riding snowboards at Perisher, my son seemed to own both knowledge and compassion. As well as his role as a police officer, in his spare time he held an important position in the rural fire brigade. I also knew he often acted as a sounding board for his friends, giving carefully reasoned advice. I leant forward and listened.

'People put shit all over us for anything from handing out speed-ing fines to shooting people who are aiming guns at other people. They don't have any idea. It's very isolating. The things we see, the stuff we deal with, most ordinary people know nothing about it. There is a world that general Australians live in and then there's this kind of parallel universe where we work.'

He wanted me to know he understood how I felt, that he under-stood my suffering. But I couldn't shift the idea that I was to blame for Wayne's death. So, my son took me home that afternoon, sat me down and questioned me again, persistently, the way police are trained to do, in order to prove to me that everything I'd done that morning had been the only option I'd had.

'What do you do when someone is in trouble?'

A nod when I answered about calling the emergency number.

'Why did you keep trying to get the ambulance?'

Another nod as I explained it was the only way to get help.

'What would have happened if you hadn't rung for the ambulance, Mum?'

I shook my head. I wasn't sure.

My patient son rephrased the question.

'What if you had just sat beside him, holding his hand while he died, instead of running and trying to get help? What if you had stayed in the room after he collapsed and attempted CPR or mouth-to-mouth? How much did Wayne weigh? Is CPR able to be properly performed if the person is lying on a mattress? How could you have got him off the bed? Didn't you say it took the two ambulance officers *and* you to eventually lift his body off the bed? The room wasn't big enough and he was simply too *big.*'

'The alternative scenario,' my son continued, 'is you still would have been sitting on that bed, Mum, beside your dead husband. You'd still be trying to perform CPR. And no ambulance would have turned up, ever. Ever!' And he punctuated his words with urgent inflection. 'At least you tried!'

'Wayne died from a heart attack, Mum. Trust me. His bad temper beforehand is one of the associated symptoms. He probably knew he wasn't well.'

But I was wrung dry with my sense of culpability. There was also something called secondary grief, my new doctor explained to me.

'Before travelling to Spain, you resigned from your career as a senior teacher? Right?' She asked me.

I nodded at the doctor, huddled in the chair in her office.

Said, with a vestige of old pride, 'I was even a relieving principal sometimes.'

'And when you left Australia, you felt confident? In love? Everything was okay because you were together, even though you'd left your whole life behind?'

I nodded again, remembering the hard-won visas, the two of us marching so trustingly away from everything we knew.

'And now,' I could hear she was trying to speak kindly, 'you're living week-to-week in someone else's house. All your furniture is borrowed. You are unemployed.' She paused again, I think to find a gentler way to say it, but there was no gentler way.

'You haven't just lost your husband, Susan.'

But there was more, so much more . . .

I explained to Di in broken telephone conversations.

'Without a proper death certificate or an official cause of death, my solicitors are saying no money will be released from the estate at all. Not in the immediate future, anyway.'

My best friend offered me cash. She offered me a loan. She thought of jobs I could do.

But I turned them down. Because all I wanted was my sense of place back—beside Wayne.

That night, seated on my mother's old couch in the little rented living room, I took a deep breath. Cheap lace curtains hung across the windows. A 40-watt globe was screwed into the light fitting—I hadn't wasted money on buying a shade. The couch was upholstered in some irritating fabric I remembered from childhood.

Beside me, in the open container, lay the dust; it was surprisingly delicate. But it was copious too. Marked amongst it were slivers and chips of small, scarred pieces of bone.

Tracing my fingers through the ash, I rubbed it between the tips of my fingers. As the chalky residue attached to my skin, I thought: *This is my husband. And I love him. And it is wondrous to touch him again and to have him close, to hold him in my hands.*

I gathered up a silver heart-shaped locket, the chain scattered about in a loose pattern across my lap as I opened it with the tips of my nails. When it was half open, lying across my thigh, I pinched some of the dust from among the silt, added a snowflake of his bone, and deposited both into the locket. *Now always*, I thought, *he will be with me, resting next to my heart, against my skin.*

Despite what the doctor had explained, I think I felt the lowest I'd ever felt. I seemed unable to crawl out of despair. There is conflict between your heart and your head, she'd said. Logically you know what has happened and logically you may be able to see what you should do to move forward, but your heart has not caught up. So, I tallied my losses daily while I ate my way through my own grief and gained twenty kilos. Devon sandwiches with tomato sauce were satisfying and cheap.

23

Morpeth, early October 2015

SIXTEEN WEEKS AFTER MY HUSBAND died, twelve weeks after I left Granada, eight weeks after the memorial service, another letter arrived from my solicitors—*Sorry Susan, but both the bank and the super fund have denied you access to any money without the full death certificate and without an official cause of death.* Probate could not commence.

Anxiety flowed through my belly. It overwhelmed me at unexpected times throughout the day. It spread and burned through my chest. Then it rose up my throat till my airways constricted. *Thump thump* was the physical pounding of my heart below my ribs, reiterating my fear day after day. The percentage of women who die from a heart attack in the first year after their husband's death is extraordinary, according to Dr Google. But I was trying—to distract myself, to follow my instincts, to do whatever was necessary to survive—to move through this half-light.

So one morning, instead of losses tallied, I counted assets. I'd visited Mum the previous weekend. It was pointless explaining to her that my husband had died and I was back for good. Instead, I cried buckets beside her while she slept, partly due to the fact that

138

she couldn't comfort me. The nurses all thought I was crying for her, and that made me cry even more.

But the visit had reminded me of words she'd been fond of repeating as I was growing up, when I was struggling to raise Jonno as a single mother: *if there's a problem, look it straight in the eye and deal with it.*

In other words, I needed to wake up to myself. My mum would've called what I was about to do 'taking stock'—making a list of all the advantages I still had in my life.

I have family and friends supporting me.
I have Wayne's ute, so I have transport.
My phone.
My books.
I have enough clothes.
My computer is loaded with all the photographs from Spain.
I have my manuscript to work on.
The computer means I can apply for work.
There is $2000 in the bank.
Mum's furniture.
Millie.
I have my teaching degree and my experience.

But, because I had resigned from teaching at the end of 2014, returning to the classroom was not an immediate option. A lengthy waiting time would be required for paperwork to be completed, interviews to be arranged and accomplished. I wasn't in a fit state to return to full-time teaching anyway. I'd been a good teacher and I didn't want to go back into a school and fail.

So, scouring the job sites on Google once again, I began to apply for work, anything to make some money: part-time receptionist positions; check-out work at Coles. One day, a woman called to inform me I had made it through to the final group of potential recruits for a government call centre position, but had failed the final psychometric test.

'Your scores demonstrated a particularly low result for "positivity".'

I actually laughed, and immediately tried something else—I invested some of my remaining nest egg in a bar course and responsible service of alcohol training. But I was dreadful! Everyone else was under twenty-five. And I couldn't stop my hands from trembling. The practical training part of the course saw me serving vodka instead of Bacardi and serving beer with a head of froth. At the end of the day the trainer took me aside and suggested I attempt to find work in the bowling clubs and RSLs. The bars and nightclubs are 'not quite the thing for you, love'.

Then unexpectedly, towards the end of October, an email from the wonderful Angela at the Australian embassy in Portugal popped into my inbox. It was now over four months since Wayne had died.

> . . . we have despatched today, to your lawyer, the original death certificate which was completed ahead of the time frame expected. Furthermore, we have received advice that the autopsy report is ready to be collected.

In twenty-four hours, I would know why Wayne had died.

Restless, I sat and watched the clock that night, unable to do anything constructive. Nine o'clock. Eleven o'clock. I checked my emails again. Ran my finger down the cord to make sure my phone was charging. At one o'clock, propped up in bed—Millie, unaware of the tension, snoring at my feet—still no report. I fell into an unsound sleep; woke at odd hours and blindly checked the phone.

Jerking awake at the first suggestion of sunlight, I reached across for my reading glasses and my phone, both nearby on the bedside table. Logged in with trembling fingers to access my emails. Made a mistake I was so tired. 'Fuck.' Millie twitched awake. Observed me curiously as I muttered and fumbled. And there was the email. There it was!

I stopped breathing.

Angela, kindly woman, directed me in her covering letter to page six of the *Certidao.*

Conclusoes:

A morte de Wayne Francis foi devida a enfarte do miocardio por ateroscle-rose das arterias coronarias cardiacas, por aterosclerose generalizada grave.

Esta e causa de morte natural.

Nao foramencontradas lesoes traumaticas recentes, exceto as devidas as manobras de reanimacao.

O exame quimico-toxicologico do sanguedo cadaver nao reveloua presencade drogas de abuso, medicamentos e de alcool.

Relief washed me clean. I slumped back against the pillow, my eyes full. It wasn't my fault. I hadn't let Wayne down. I grabbed Millie and buried my face in her neck and cried and cried.

Page after page of autopsy and toxicology results revealed that Wayne had died from a myocardial infarction due to blocked arter-ies. His main coronary arteries were severely blocked. All the other arteries were seriously compromised. His death was from completely natural causes.

No matter how fast I had run, no matter where I had run to, no matter if that number I so frantically and repeatedly and pointlessly dialled had connected with someone, it would not have made any difference. Even if we'd been in New South Wales, the chances of my husband's survival would have been low.

Running for an ambulance was exactly the right thing to do because only an ambulance, its crew and its equipment would have saved him. What an ordinary, rather simple death, for my extraordinary man.

Part 3

Finding Myself

2016–2018

24

Newcastle, autumn 2016

THE ESTATE WAS FINALLY SETTLED in March. Feeling both guilt and relief that I was now able to afford a place of my own, I worked from instinct and bought a small cottage in an inner-city suburb of Newcastle. Traditionally a working-class area where coal dust from BHP had made the streets dirty and unpopular for more than half a century, Mayfield was now creeping towards a disorderly kind of gentrification.

The hospital where Enid had given birth to me was two kilometres down the road. The caravan park where she and O'Connor had stayed during the week leading up to my delivery was now a dumpsite next to a disused railway line in the semi-industrial suburb of Hexham, ten minutes away. The irony did not go unnoticed. I'd come back to where I'd started.

People warned me about Mayfield: the drugs, the crime and the wildness. Driving Wayne's ute up and down the narrow streets on the Saturday morning before I moved in, I watched elderly neighbours shuffle about on walkers and the young professional couple next door painting their front door, the radio blaring through an open window. Youths addicted to a variety of substances rode by on undersized pushbikes to visit the empty lot beside the railway station. They were frighteningly focused, intent on nothing but their destination. On the main street I watched people walking in and out of the pawnbrokers; I watched young mothers decked out in active-wear pushing babies in buggies, on a quest to buy imported cheese from the most expensive delicatessen in Newcastle. Cafes lined the road into the city. Nothing fitted together; nobody slotted in place. The demographics of the suburb were scattered like pieces from an upended jigsaw. But I felt I fitted, amongst all the unfitted.

When Di and I had first inspected the house, despite the presence of the real estate agent, I cried. Di felt it too, and clutched my arm, 'This is it.'

A 1920s Californian bungalow with a working fireplace, sash windows in the bedrooms, polished floorboards throughout and featuring fine stained glass: it was everything I wanted; everything I believed I needed. There were three bedrooms, a patch of yard and verandas running front and back. The atmosphere in the house was quiet and calm. And although I didn't know it at the time, this was important, because I was going to need some solitude. The gods hadn't finished with their reckoning yet.

'It feels surreal, Di.'

We were sitting on the front steps the morning after moving day. The small amount of worldly goods I owned were still packed in boxes, except for some mugs she'd given me as a house-warming present, the kettle and the coffee. A single bottle of milk stood open on the kitchen sink.

'His death and this place,' I indicated the space around us, 'are intrinsically linked. If he hadn't died, we wouldn't be sitting here.'

My best friend took my hand and said, for the thousandth time, 'and that's okay, amigo. Because he would want you to be safe and happy.'

Slowly, a structure for my new life emerged. I bought a queen-sized bed, two couches and, finally, a washing machine and fridge. I wrote daily on the laptop at the new kitchen table, racing to finish my book. I entered short story competitions and subscribed to literary magazines. One of my former students from out west came to stay with me on her break from studying at the University of New England. Wayne's cousin and his wife turned up for Sunday lunch. Martha and her partner Jack spent a few days with me before they headed off on a trek to Western Australia, towing a caravan. 'Why Newcastle?' everyone asked. 'Why not return to Dubbo?'

'Because of the people,' I said.

Di was living here. Jonno worked two hours away, in Sydney. Pete and his family owned a house a few suburbs away. And even though Liz's eldest daughter Caitlin was working in Canberra, Ashleigh, her younger sister, was studying at the University of Newcastle. Mum lived in a local nursing home. Damien, a dizzyingly gay friend from a job years ago, had returned to the town and gave me decorating advice, while Gai, my old boss, steered me towards the decent coffee shops. I wasn't a hundred per cent certain about where my place was now, but I didn't really know where else to go.

It was Pete and Jan who suggested I offer English lessons from home, 'just to tide you over, Suz, till you know what you want to do'. I used some of the money Wayne had left me to pay for the creation of a logo; applied for an ABN. I met with some tech heads and they developed a website. Gradually, I built up a client base combining students studying for their HSC, small children learning how to read and primary students transitioning to high school; it kept me afloat.

I also joined a writing group and the time I spent with other writers became the most important part of my week. It was the writing, the conversations we had about each other's work, that I credit for allowing me to experience happiness again. It focused me. I wrote about Wayne; I wrote about our love and I wrote about my grief. I was lucky enough to have a couple of short stories published. I worked on finishing my book. And that's how I began to rebuild my life and myself.

Millie, my little terrier, who'd been so faithful for so long, finally had to be put to sleep. Such was her tenacity that she still wagged her tail at the idea of a walk, even though both her back legs had given way. I was sad, but it was not the degree of sadness I'd expected; it seemed nothing would ever be quite so sad for me again.

Mum languished in her nursing home, lifeless in her chair, seeing and understanding nothing. She had outlived my dad, my dog, my best friend and my husband. Nobody visited her anymore—except Pete and me, and sometimes Jan or Di. The nurses lifted her into bed; showered her on a trolley, fed her mash off a spoon. That she was still alive, in such an undignified way, while Wayne and Liz were dead, was something I found difficult to reconcile. The incongruity made me both resentful and unhappy. Liz would have given anything to live another day. To watch her girls grow up. To be with Geoff. And Wayne, it seemed to me, had so few years of happiness. He deserved more.

And yet here was Mum, still alive.

Ashleigh was a regular visitor to my house, often dropping in to have a cup of tea or a meal, with stories about her classes, her bar job, university life. She was studying social work and we spent long afternoons on the veranda in the winter sun, discussing refugees, euthanasia, my grief, her own sorrow.

One afternoon she told me about a new topic she was studying—the continuing bonds of grief. She stared into her teacup, then glanced up, eyes bright and beautiful, reminding me so much of Liz.

'Death doesn't always alter the attachment people who are grieving feel for the person who's died. Psychologists say people can consciously choose to continue the bond they have with their deceased,' Ashleigh said.

'That makes sense', I replied. 'I think Di and I have chosen to continue our relationship with your mum. I know I still talk to her on occasion. But Wayne is different somehow. I still love Wayne as much as I did when we moved to Granada. But it doesn't seem to me—right now—that I have any kind of choice about whether or not to continue my relationship with him. I can't *stop* loving him. That's what makes it so difficult. It's hard loving someone when it's such a one-sided affair.'

Ashleigh shifted in her chair, her eyes met mine again. 'Everyone comes into your life for a reason. What's that quote from *Four Weddings and a Funeral*? That the big gay guy says at the Scottish wedding? Something about let us all be proud to be able to say, we too were once adored?'

With those words sounding in my ears, I kept working at my grief—as the blogs and articles I read suggested. I wrote and wrote. I exercised at the gym with Bruce, my new trainer. I made myself go out with friends. Made new friends. I invited people into my home and worked hard at building up the tutoring business—no matter how I sometimes felt—no matter that the heartache swelled inside me and I thought I'd go crazy if I didn't open my mouth and scream at the sky. The desperate need to be with Wayne, to talk with him and to feel his hand in the small of my lower back stayed with me, always. I began to hate my grief—or was it my love? I couldn't escape from it.

Wendy, a new friend, whose opinion I valued, suggested I read the books Joan Didion and Joyce Carol Oates had written, about their experiences following the deaths of their husbands. And afterwards, I felt a little better. Some of their experiences were my experiences. I recognised my anger, my sense of desolation and hopelessness, my craziness. The insight I gained reminded me of what I'd written to Wayne about reading, about books making more sense than the world around me: *as a girl, I found that what was written in books was more familiar to me than what I experienced in the real world.*

Towards the end of Oates' book, she describes a morning, about twelve months after her husband died, when she is trying to clean up the garbage spilled on the driveway by some racoons. She spots an earring she was missing. It wasn't a particularly valuable or sentimental piece of jewellery. But Oates experiences a moment of enlightenment. She understands from this incident that her life will now be lived amongst loss, and challenge, but that sometimes, she might still discover moments of happiness.

It was both a dreadful idea and a liberating idea: life would never again be the bright endless stretch of possibility it had once been, but at least sometimes, between each hopeless horizon, I might be able to discover a little light.

But life never plays out the way you expect.

25

Mayfield, January 2017

'HOP UP ON THE BED,' she said, in that cheerful voice doctors use that always makes my heart sink: undies down, it means. In this case, roll onto your belly while I examine your private folds and creases and embarrassing bits. After that, she didn't say very much. Except that she would be away in Sri Lanka on holidays for two weeks visiting family and would speak to me when she returned. She did. And I was never more surprised in all my life. The irony seemed almost equal to Wayne dying—after travelling to Spain so we could 'live'.

I'd caught herpes from my dead husband.

We'd never had a discussion about either one of us carrying this disease. I'd never even given sexually transmitted diseases a second thought. Why would I? The medical clearances we'd received so we could settle in Spain included mandatory STD checks. It was only now that I discovered genital herpes could go undiagnosed for years unless the lesions—a hideous word, yet one that perfectly summed up how I felt—were active.

This seemed yet another payback for the joy Wayne and I shared—because we'd believed we could simply pick pleasure like

151

an apple off a tree. Apparently, I'd not yet sacrificed enough. Now I had herpes. And I was infected for life. Any chance of moving forward from all this grief seemed unfeasible. Being loved again? Belonging to anyone else? No chance. I was living with the mark of my dead husband.

It had been back in March 2015—three months into our life in Granada—when I'd first been worried, in a vague kind of way, about a strange sensation on my bum. It was an uncomfortable feeling. Tingly. Painful. And the blisters I could touch, but not see, were taking weeks to clear up. An infection of some kind?

Then, a month and a half later, the tenderness resurfaced, as did the as-yet-unseen sores. I remember twisting in the bathroom one morning, poking my phone in between my legs, to capture a photo of what I couldn't quite glimpse in the mirror. Studying the image, enlarging it while I perched naked on the side of the cement bath, shivering in the European winter, I was horrified. The blisters I'd been gingerly examining with my fingers had felt raised and raw, but I'd had no comprehension, before seeing the photo, of how ghastly they looked. I scrubbed my fingers obsessively under water from the tap. What on earth was it?

Later, hunched in a chair at the breakfast table beside the French doors, as the Spanish sunlight filtered into our little living room, I edited the picture on my phone with my thumb and fore-finger until only the image of the sores was visible. I could now safely show this picture to the pharmacist downtown and ask her advice.

I trundled down the still, cobblestone alleyways to the streets of Granada, hands stuffed into my black duffle coat against the freezing cold, while my husband still snored contentedly in bed under the feather-down doona—and proffered my phone to the chemist, pointing out the *mucho problema*. As poor as my Spanish was,

I understood I needed to apply the ointment four times a day. She didn't provide a diagnosis.

After a week, the pain disappeared. 'Your bum looks better, my love,' Wayne grinned, as I hopped naked out of our bed, eager to explore that particular, sweet Spanish morning. And that was that. Because the lemon-coloured delight of living in the south of Europe, then the sorrow that fell around me later, made blisters a small concern. I never thought it might be a sexually transmitted disease. I had imagined the tight shapewear I was using to look like the beautiful Spanish women surrounding me had cut my skin and somehow that had become infected. So, it was only once I was living in Mayfield, after the visit to my lovely doctor, that I wondered about the ease with which Wayne had reassured me.

'But how? Why didn't he say something to me?' I sniffed to the doctor. 'And why didn't I get it when we first started seeing each other? Couldn't I have picked it up from somebody else? Before him?'

'It's possible your husband didn't know,' the doctor said, passing me another tissue. 'Men often don't get their symptoms as severely as women do. Possibly he contracted it when he was young and hadn't had a recurrence in decades. Initial symptoms appear a week to two weeks after the first infection. Sometimes the symptoms never return. Usually not as severe as the first bout anyway. Unfortunately, that's not the situation in your case.' She paused. Turned her back to me. Washed her hands under the sink and dried them with a paper towel. Faced me again, her dark eyes sympathetic. 'Possibly he knew, but didn't want to tell you?'

And immediately I thought back—to that black night in Lisbon, three days after Wayne had died, and the unexpected sharpness of a ringtone. Jonno, frowning across the room at me, his finger pausing the play button on the video he was watching. I thought back to how later I'd deliberately pushed the disembodied voice, insinuating there were things I didn't know about my husband, to the back of my mind. Because there was too much to deal with already.

Herpes was about to become the least of my problems. And even my grief for Wayne would seem a simpler burden.

There were still secrets to unravel.

26

Lisbon, June 2015

WHEN JONNO HAD ARRIVED THAT day, on a plane from Australia, I remember standing at the top of the stairs watching my son make his way towards me, sports bag slung across one shoulder. I felt a profound calmness. At last, some sense of the familiar had returned. I thanked God that I'd borne a boy who'd grown up to be my friend, and a man I could rely on.

'Mum,' he said simply, and we hugged tight.

I ushered him down the concrete hallway into the one-bedroom flat Wayne and I had been renting in Lisbon. It was a cold, square box of a place.

Jonno was still smoking back then, but the apartment was smoke-free. So, as I relayed the story of all my interminable running around, the phones refusing to work, the woman across the way standing powerless in the doorway of her apartment, the long manner of my husband's death, Jonno's hand dangled out the open window, a cigarette clutched between two fingers, the curl of smoke circling into the Portuguese air. He sat opposite me and talked me through everything, step by step. He forced me to repeat parts. He

155

explained aspects of the process to me. At the end he said, 'Mum, what else could you have done?'

We spent the remainder of the day trudging from one end of Lisbon to the other, filling in time, the city still turning despite Wayne's death. I was exhausted, but it was a wide-eyed tiredness. The glare of the Portuguese summer had curved into pink dusk. We were back in the apartment and my clever son was playing an action movie DVD on his computer, trying to distract me. But we had it turned up too loud and the people in the next flat banged on the wall in a series of sudden thumps. I leapt up in fright.

Then my phone rang.

I didn't recognise the number. I glanced at Jonno.

'Answer it,' he smiled. 'It's okay, Mum.'

'Susan?'

'Yes?'

'This is David. From Rome. Wayne's cousin.'

And I thought, *Mmmm*, to myself, while I picked through the seconds, playing for time. For this was the cousin Wayne had not spoken to in fifteen years. Something about a bust-up when Wayne's father, Stan, had died. We'd talked about going to visit this man while we were in Spain. David had married an Italian girl and they ran a cafe somewhere on the outskirts of the grand old Roman capital. Flights from Madrid to Rome were cheap. My husband was considering trying to make amends for old troubles.

'I heard about Wayne's death. I'm shocked. I wanted to ring and give you my condolences.'

A gunshot cracked from the video Jonno was watching.

I replied mechanically. 'Thank you very much. Everyone is stunned. It's very unexpected.'

'There was no indication? You never had any warning?'

I distinctly heard, behind his voice, the lid being screwed off a bottle, liquid spilling into a glass over clinking ice cubes.

'Nothing. No idea.' I listened more carefully, pressing the phone tight to my ear, and heard him gulp down whatever it was he was drinking.

'I can't believe it. Wayne, of all people. I thought he was indestructible, the old bastard.' The man already sounded a little drunk.

By now, Jonno was looking at me questioningly through the flickering light reflecting off the screen. I mimed an 'I dunno' action with my spare hand.

'Put it on speaker phone,' he whispered. And I did, because I was suspicious.

'And you're his wife?'

For a moment, anger surged through me so fast and hot I thought I would vomit. 'Yes,' in my coldest, proudest voice. 'We married last year.'

'Can't believe the old arsehole finally got married. He never did before, you know? Not once. Always declared he wouldn't. Didn't believe in it. But I reckon it's more that no one would have him. Him being married is almost as big a bombshell as him bloody dying.'

'We were very much in love. He was the greatest man I ever met.'

'Wayne? You're kidding me?'

I raised my eyebrows again at Jonno.

'So, what kind of work do you do?' he continued. 'How'd you meet him? How long had you known him before you got hitched?' And that's when it started to feel like an interrogation.

Jonno pulled a strange face at me. He was sitting up straighter on his chair, hand extended out the window again.

'What on earth were you doing in Spain?' David's voice interrupted my thoughts. 'Last I heard, he was working underground in Kalgoorlie. He never liked to raise his head above dirt level.

157

Understandable. It was a good way of disappearing.' Disbelievingly, I heard the glass being filled up again, the smooth fall of fluid convincing me it was a spirit of some kind.

Explaining all the reasons we'd left Australia, I deliberately peppered my account with words like 'adored' and 'devotion'. I was staking my claim, laying out my loyalty.

'We wanted to experience different cultures. Learn the language. Have this great adventure together.'

David hooted. 'Wayne? I don't believe it.' I opened my eyes up wide at Jonno who had now relaxed again in his fold-out chair, half watching me, half watching the computer screen. He shrugged. It was up to me if I wanted to continue this discussion.

'You sound like a sweet woman,' David said, changing the direction of the conversation. 'I've seen your Facebook photographs. Compared to the old boy you look like a stiff breeze would blow you over. How on earth did someone like you end up marrying him?'

Dazed, I didn't know what to say. *Didn't he know Wayne?* Everyone who was even vaguely acquainted with my husband admired and respected him. Everyone understood immediately why I'd married him. How on earth could I *not* have married him? He was generous in spirit. Intelligent. Tall and strong. He was a good man who loved me.

'Hang on a minute. I've got to take a leak.'

And the voice on the end of the phone line disappeared.

'Mum you don't have to talk to this guy, you know. What he's saying is totally inappropriate. And to be saying it to you *today*? Doesn't he have any respect?' Jonno shook his head, paused the movie. 'I'd hang up.'

'Yep, okay. I will. As soon as he gets back.'

But I never had the opportunity. The conversation dragged on for at least another hour. And to my mind, the purpose appeared to be David's need to satisfy his own disbelief. He couldn't quite fathom how Wayne had finally married. Or why I'd married him. Or that he'd really died. He seemed intent on proving a certain perspective he held about my husband. And I, in my grief, was equally certain I had to prove the opposite.

'I don't understand, Susan,' he was slurring his words. 'Why did you marry him? You're pretty and so tiny.' I *was*, back then. But I couldn't quite grasp the significance of why the man kept referring to the difference in our physical sizes. And the sloppier he became with alcohol, the slimier were his insinuations.

'You're a sexy woman. Gorgeous girl. You look gorgeous.' He was almost incoherent. 'Why with him? Of all people?'

'One reason is because he always made me feel safe. Some of the experiences I've had in the past with men were not so great. Wayne made me feel like I was being taken care of.'

And again, I heard that incredulous hoot of laughter. Another gunshot snapped out from the video. I heard the wailing of women.

'*He* made you feel safe? You obviously didn't know a lot about the secrets from his past. Didn't he tell you about his father? Didn't he talk about the way he grew up? What Stan was like?'

Responding in detail, as I felt I must, because it was like some examination I had to pass to prove the love I'd shared with Wayne had been real, I explained all I knew. About Wayne's childhood. About Stan's suicide. Not that Wayne had ever spoken in detail about it. I lifted up my chin. Take that! And yes, it silenced David for a while. Then I heard him pour himself more liquor.

'Fair enough. But answer me this. Did he ever tell you the real reason why he had to leave New Guinea? Go to Australia? Why he had to change his surname? Why he never went back to the Highlands?'

'He said he wanted to get away from his father,' I replied. 'That Australia offered him more opportunity. He said that when he started working in the mines, there was some other guy who had the same surname as him. So, he changed his own name.'

On the other end of the line, David laughed.

'Well, you didn't really know your husband at all. Not even a little bit. He lied to you. When you find out the truth about what that violent bastard did, talk to me then about how much you love him.'

And he hung up.

27

Mayfield, May 2017

'YES, IT'S TRUE,' MARTHA HAD said to me, her hands clenched together in despair, her eyes unable to meet mine. She was perched on the edge of the lounge, shaking her head like she wanted to deny the words coming out of her mouth. Our weekend to catch up—for Martha and her Jack to share with me their road trip around Australia—hadn't quite worked out according to anybody's plans.

'Oh, Suz. We discussed whether to tell you or not when Wayne first started seeing you. He didn't know what to do. I didn't know what to do.'

My heart constricted.

'Both of us were worried it would scare you off, and he already understood you were the girl for him.' Martha's breathing was ragged between her tears. When she glanced up at me, her face so beaten, I took one step back.

'I guess in the end he kept the truth from you for too long. He didn't want to risk losing you. He was afraid that if you knew the truth you wouldn't love him anymore.'

It had happened in New Guinea, she told me. In the remote region of the Highlands. In a lawless town, amongst the screech of parrots and the torrential rains—back when Wayne was in his early twenties, wild and privileged because of his youth and the colour of his skin. Two very different accounts existed about the night. There was Martha's version, and there were questions that remained on the public record. I knew there was no such thing as absolute truth. But what Martha was telling me completely refused to mesh with the man I'd known.

But what could I do? Because now, of course, my husband was dead. All the questions I wanted to ask him had to remain unasked. And New Guinea was a violent place—a place he'd told me a thousand times he'd never take me. A place his mother had warned me about, including stories of being ambushed and shot at. A place the Department of Foreign Affairs posted a permanent warning about, encouraging travellers to use 'a high degree of caution'.

After Martha and Jack left, heading for home, my confusion and preoccupation with what I'd been told multiplied—secrets were something I loathed. I yearned to fly to Goroka and pull someone towards me by the front of their soaked, sweaty shirt and demand a satisfactory response. I hankered to fly to this mythical place of my husband's childhood: to see, to understand; to feel the thump of dancing feet under my own, hear the cries of the birds, the smell of burnt sweet potato cooking behind the walls of corrugated iron sheds.

Equally, I was unsure about it being my business. This had been something Wayne had deliberately chosen to keep hidden. When I questioned Silas later in the week on the phone, the nephew Wayne had loved as a son said the incident had almost killed *his* father John.

'It's not something my family talk about.'

No one was willing to talk and I became a little unwilling to ask. But unconditionally loving a dead man, living with the worst sort of unanswered questions, wasn't something I had the capacity to endure.

Di and I were lazing in the white cane chairs on the back veranda, in the winter sunlight. It was a breezy, Sunday morning and the pigeons hooted over our heads on my tin roof. The plumbago quivered like a purple cloud above the lawn.

'My heart still swells every time I think of him—despite what Martha's told me. But not knowing the truth—I'm not sure I can live with *that*.'

Di sipped her coffee.

'Why can't I just be content with the memories . . . and put all these questions aside? Do what Wayne always wanted? Leave the past in the past.' I ran my fingers through my hair, pushed it back out of my face.

My best friend set her apple muffin down on the rickety wicker table, her mug of coffee beside it, taking a moment to balance the table with two hands, and then she stretched across to take my hand.

'The idea of him keeping that stuff a secret from me breaks my heart.' I shook her fingers free, refused to be comforted *again*. I was so tired of the sorry state of my life—of how it felt like bad things were being done *to* me.

'Thirty years underground, hiding away from the world for that one terrible mistake he made when he was young. Or the mistake he didn't make? I thought I understood the unhappiness from his childhood. I thought it was all about his father. But this revelation takes it to a whole different level!' I shook my head. 'I still can't believe it. I can't believe it really happened. I don't believe he would do such a thing.'

Di was silent. She took her time zipping up the baby blue jacket she'd bought for sailing on the lake; she often felt the cold.

'Wayne was such a proud man. I guess I get why he didn't tell you. And I get why you want answers about whether he did or didn't do it. But this on top of his death, the herpes diagnosis, starting over again from scratch: it's all just too much, Suz. No wonder you're confused.' Then she sat up straighter, turned her gaze from the garden to me. Took up her coffee again, her blue eyes noticeably harder.

'I just wish you'd never been told about it in the first place.' She frowned at me. Then she shook her head, as if to shake the past from both of us.

'Di . . .' I interrupted, 'I asked about it. I asked Martha about what David was talking about. I asked because in the back of my mind, all this time, I knew something wasn't right. After the Herpes diagnosis. After the hints David gave me. I just wasn't ready to know. Up until now. Because too much else was going on.'

'Well,' she humphed, 'it was pointless. You've got enough to deal with already. Why did your dreams have to be shattered like that?'

28

Mayfield, August 2017

MARTHA'S REVELATION EXPLAINED WHAT DAVID had been referring to that night on the phone in Lisbon. But the hard truth was that Martha was Wayne's mother. The little she'd told me was simply not enough; it was nowhere near enough. I needed an objective account.

That August wasn't a great month. But I battled through it, questions and partially made decisions racing through my head. It was the term immediately preceding the HSC and some of my senior students, as much as I loved them, were testy or despairing or over-eager, or all of those things combined.

'Should I use the thesis I did in my trial or write a new one?'

'Susan, do you think the Tim Winton short story is the best related text for me to use?'

'My teacher said I need to rewrite my creative narrative. She said to use a flashback. The examiners like to see a flashback.'

Making the decision to investigate what had happened in New Guinea in 1978 bloomed out of all this chaos.

The afternoon Martha had told me, she'd been overwhelmed with emotion. Jack had strolled in—he'd been waiting out the back on the veranda, ostensibly reading the paper—and led her to the spare room, insisting she needed to lie down and rest. I'd waited for a little while in the sudden silence of the house. Breathed. In. Out. Bent my face towards my heart. Searched myself for breakages. How did I feel? It was insane, wasn't it? During a perceptible space of time that afternoon, like a painting washed to white, I wasn't present in the world. For a long while after that day, I felt like I'd been smashed over the head.

I stood up stiffly, like I was a hundred years old. To give my emotions space, I needed to leave the house. My face was set; I was trying to act as if this was all okay, to spare Martha's feelings. But inside my heart everything had been ripped to shreds.

I drove automatically, to the shops at Waratah, my arms rigid in front of me. I was in shock, and the world seemed a long way away. I'd parked Wayne's ute in the carpark—to be alone, to think—to absorb what I'd been told. To try and simply comprehend this unfathomable thing.

I remember glancing out the window in despair and realising, with a start, that the car next to me was moving! Without a driver. I know my forehead wrinkled in confusion for one long second. It was a pale blue SUV, it was sliding past my car . . . in slow motion. Empty. How could that be? But shit. Suddenly I understood—it was me! I hadn't pulled the handbrake on properly. *My* car was sliding—backwards. Thank God it was a Saturday afternoon and the carpark was half empty.

In that moment, I knew I had to comprehend what this secret meant to me, to move forward. Unless I understood the event, I'd never be able to absorb it. I was still in shock but I recognised already that I would be unable to live with a version of Wayne that was so at odds with the man who I loved, and who I believed had loved me. If what Martha was telling me had happened, was anything we'd shared the way I remembered it? Granada had been the most extraordinary time of my life. Belonging to Wayne had given me such a strong sense of who I was. But if he wasn't the man I had thought him to be, if he'd kept such a crucial secret from me, some of the foundations I'd built my identity around were made of straw.

At the beginning of August, I decided one thing I could do was call Liz's eldest daughter, Caitlin, who was a solicitor.

Curling up on the sofa in the lounge room proper, in what I called the 'formal' room, I folded my knees under me and took a deep breath. My fingers were shaking. I gazed from the fireplace, the elegant wooden 1930s mantelpiece, to the Art Deco stained-glass window arched above the front doorway. Late-afternoon sun was glistening through the coloured glass, creating flickers like grassfire sparks. The blue glass teardrops seemed to melt like wax down the leadlight panes.

I rang Caitlin and she got straight to the point. 'Aunty Sue. Is everything all right?'

'It's fine, baby. I just needed to talk to you about some stuff.'

I could imagine her sitting on the edge of her couch in the apartment she'd bought off plan, in one of the satellite suburbs on the edge of old Canberra. My Caitie was like that. Clear-headed. Ambitious. Clever. She called a spade a spade. Didn't like to waste time. Liz had often bemoaned not knowing where Caitlin had come from. Because in character Liz had been very much the opposite— cautious and conciliatory. But she'd been proud of Caitlin's strength and intelligence. And that was why my nickname for Caitlin was Love Child. Because if I'd ever had a daughter, I would have wanted her to be just like Caitlin. When Caitlin and I laughed, both of us would laugh so hard we would end up suffering identical asthma attacks, wheezing and whistling while we rolled about.

Caitlin's partner, Rose, was, by the strangest twist of fate, originally from New Guinea. And that Caitlin understood the law was more than a little advantageous.

'There's something I found out about Wayne's past. Just recently. Something he never told me. And the story is just so at odds with the man I knew. I need you to help me discover the truth.' I choked then. And she gave me silence so I could recover.

'There was a verdict handed down in New Guinea. Years and years ago. I need your professional opinion about how the trial proceeded. Whether you think things were handled properly. Fairly.' I gasped at air. 'If you can't help me Caitie, I don't know what else to do.'

I sighed. The more I verbalised it, the more real it became. Jonno now knew. Di knew. Pete and Ashleigh.

'Yes?' For once my beautiful Caitie sounded wary.

Resorting to clichés, because I had no idea how to tell her such a thing without being face to face, 'This will come as a bit of a shock, hun.'

She was as patient as always. Level-headed. 'It's okay. Just tell me. Just come out with it and tell me.'

I always recognised, somewhere inside myself, that there was more to the story than I'd been told. I'd faltered when David asked me if I'd known why Wayne had first come to Australia. I *had* asked Wayne one night, when we were still living in Dubbo, because I knew, despite the abuse he'd suffered as a child, that the Highlands were his first love and that he sorely missed his brother, the people he'd grown up with, the freedom he'd enjoyed.

'How come you came here and John stayed behind?' But I hadn't pressed Wayne too hard. I'd accepted his half-hearted response at face value. My worst imaginings were perhaps he'd been fired from a job. Maybe he'd beaten another man up in a bar brawl. Had his father disowned him?

I cleared my throat and pressed the phone hard against my ear. My house was quiet. Waiting.

'Back in 1978,' I said, 'Wayne was charged with murder. In a court in the Highlands.'

Even the unflappable Caitlin was shocked into an almost silence. 'What?'

'In 1978, in Goroka, the police alleged Wayne murdered the young woman he was living with. An appeal meant the charge was reduced to manslaughter. He was sentenced to three years in gaol.'

'How do you know all this?'

'His mother told me, a little while ago. Then I did some research. I found an old Trove article with the news report.' And I read aloud from the article.

Friday 17 Nov 1978

PORT MORESBY, Thursday (AAP).—An Australian who killed a young woman in a domestic argument was sentenced to three years' jail in Goroka yesterday after being found guilty of manslaughter.

[The accused] had originally been charged with murder.

Mr Justice Pritchard said the death of Miss Caroline Benny, 21, from Losuia, in the Trobriand Islands, had occurred in distressing circumstances during an emotionally violent scene.

'I need your help, Caitie. I need to find the truth about what happened.'

29

Mayfield, August 2017

THAT NIGHT, HALF-LYING ON THE couch after I'd wished Caitlin goodnight, I began sifting through my memories, searching for answers. Where once it had been a re-enactment of the conversation between Enid and me in Brisbane, or a detailed examination of what my father had said in the Durty Nelly, or trying to piece together my own actions during those panicked moments following Wayne's death, I now scrutinised what I knew about my husband. I recalled he'd once said: 'Which story from the past ever tells us the truth about someone?'

It wasn't as if I couldn't imagine my husband killing someone. That's the appalling thing: I *could* imagine it. Only too easily. Not that I believed he would ever do it intentionally, but I knew his incredible strength. His formidable shoulders, his unbreakable back, his inability to gauge his own power. How many times had I heard him tell the story of attempting to hoist an old girlfriend onto his shoulders, and before he knew it, she was flying right over the top of his head and landing three or four metres behind him on the grass? The number of times in Granada, in an attempt to save me from stumbling into the ubiquitous dog poo, he'd shoved me to the side of the pavement at the last minute, and I'd been terrified I'd go sailing over the stone wall and land in the river below? And his temper? I remember how he'd said to me when we'd first met, 'One thing I always try to do is to never lose my temper. I hate, loathe, to lose my temper.'

I'd wondered over those words, because at that stage I'd never witnessed his temper. But when I thought about Wayne's ability to kill someone, when I thought about it consciously and impartially, memories that, when viewed in isolation, or from the time before I learnt what happened in 1978, had meant nothing, suddenly started shaping an unwelcome impression. I remembered Pete telling me a story after the memorial service, a story that one of the miners who worked with Wayne had told him at the wake.

Wayne had been sitting at the bar at one of his favourite pubs in Kalgoorlie. Everyone knew to leave Wayne alone after work, especially if he was sitting on his own. He'd told them all often enough: work was work and the pub was the pub and he didn't want the two to mix. Well, anyway, one night this new fella hadn't listened to him. Wayne told him a few times to leave him alone. That he wanted to be on his own. Old mate still didn't listen. So, Wayne turned around on his stool, and without a word, laid him out on the floor with one mighty punch. Then went back to drinking his beer.

When Pete shared this anecdote with me, he'd been laughing about it. I think he was trying to make me smile; to show me how much the guys who'd worked for Wayne respected him.

I also recalled the time we were driving through the Pyrenees. Wayne was on edge. Driving for so many days on the wrong side of the road had wearied him. Despite his proud talk of being a 'Highlands Highway' driver, the unfamiliar conditions, an unknown road, road signs in French, combined with long days and probably his flagging health, made him testy. He was, after all, a few weeks off turning sixty, but he still behaved like he was twenty. We were trailing behind a bike rider on a steep, narrow, twisty part of the road. It was impossible to see what was ahead of us, or behind us, because the turns in the road were so tight. Wayne was becoming impatient because he was forced to drive so slowly behind the guy on the mountain bike.

Then suddenly, 'Fuck,' my husband bellowed and, yanking the wheel, he veered the car sharply around the bike, roaring past the rider, inches from the man. It was a miracle the guy was not knocked off or run over. In the rear-view mirror, I watched the bike rider wobble, regain his balance, scream and raise his fist in the air at us, as Wayne continued driving, unmoved.

On that day, I'd been genuinely shocked, unable to speak. I sat in the front seat of the car trying to assemble my thoughts, as the French mountains rushed past. This behaviour was not what I was used to. The story about punching the guy in the pub had also shocked me—but only upon reflection, and when I added it to other stories.

These incidents demonstrated the wild side of my husband. I'd often romanticised it, but it now seemed lit by an emerging reality. The memories, these stories, made me anxious. I worried that Martha's version of Caroline's death was a sanitised edition. What if it was worse than what she'd said? How could I be sure I'd been told the whole truth?

But despite all the half-truths, I never, ever, was tempted to ignore this knowledge about my husband's past. The only way I could fully be me, in the present, was to know the truth of what had gone before. If I didn't find out the circumstances of Caroline's death, *my* story wouldn't be whole. Because you can't un-know information.

That night, before bed, I stood and I stretched; I wandered across to the mantelpiece and on tiptoes traced the photograph of my husband's face with my finger. I knew this man. Loved him still. Hated myself for what I was about to do next.

30

Mayfield, August 2017

WAYNE HAD TOLD ME I was never to visit New Guinea. But in a
new spirit of independence, I decided to defy that advice. Yes, the
Highlands was a violent place, I didn't need reminding of that, but
what was I supposed to do? I needed to locate John. Because if I
didn't talk to him, I would have to accept what little I knew.

Paradoxically, my crazy idea of travelling to Goroka made my
future seem almost hopeful. Because, for the first time in a long
time, I had a purpose. A purpose that somehow made it easier for
me to recognise myself again.

I'd also had a dream, since Wayne's memorial sevice, to scatter his
ashes from the summit of the mountain over the Highlands Highway.
It was his favourite place in the world. In a weird way, I believed I
could make up for not saving his life in Granada if I did this for him.
That perhaps he could forgive me for not being practical enough to
get an ambulance in time. No matter what the official reports stated,
or what the doctor said, or what Jonno said, somewhere in my irrational mind, a small part of my grief had me believing, would always
have me believing, that I should have done more.

Somehow, if I could get him home, to the one place in the world where he'd really belonged, then his past and his present would finally be connected and he could have some peace. It was also the only way I felt I could put his soul to rest. He'd died holding onto his terrible secret, and had never been able to return to his home because of it. Once again, I was reminded of our time in Spain and how many people believed the country could not be restored because its secrets were still hidden. I needed Wayne to know that I still loved him unconditionally. If I did this brave thing for him, I could help his spirit rest and at the same time strengthen my own.

Being a widow had changed me. I was not willing to take risks anymore. My world had shrunk, and my personality with it. I didn't like myself anymore. The grief I'd felt for Liz had made me rush out into the world, anxious to do everything and see everything. Travelling with Wayne, I now realised, had been a part of my reaction to her death. Now, after his death, I was settling. But I wasn't ready to settle just yet. I felt travelling to New Guinea might give me back some belief in who I was.

The following Monday, I began to ring around. And the more people I spoke to, the more details I managed to iron out, the more excited I became. I *could* do this!

Anne at Air Niugini was amazing.

'I've done this myself, Susan. You can take your husband's ashes on the plane as carry-on luggage, as long as you have the certification proving it is human ashes and all the original paperwork.'

I said, 'Since he died in Portugal, two years ago, I've undone the original seal on the container that held his ashes.'

'Then you need to get a funeral home or a crematorium to verify the ashes you now hold *are* human remains and have them resealed officially. I honestly don't think there will be any issues. It will go smoothly.'

175

Even though she couldn't see me, I bowed my head in gratitude. The kindness of strangers that I remembered from Lisbon was
beginning all over again.

Next, I rang a funeral home, close by in Mayfield.

'Unfortunately, we can't verify the ashes. We don't have those
kinds of facilities.' They directed me to a local crematorium.

'As long as you have your original paperwork you will be fine.
Just take that with you and place the ashes in a zip-lock bag inside a
container,' the man from the crematorium said. I laughed. He probably thought I was very rude. The ignorance I'd experienced on my
journey home from Spain was also beginning to kick off again, as
was my irritation.

'Look, I don't think that's enough,' I said, refusing to allow him
to convince me of something I knew was wrong.

'When I brought my husband home from Portugal the process
was very strict, very regimented. I believe the container needs to
be resealed. I think I need to be able to prove I'm carrying human
remains and nothing else. I need a certificate.'

'No, no,' he tried to assure me. But I knew he was incorrect.

In the afternoon, I looked up the number of a local travel agent.

'I'm just going to explain this a little,' I warned. 'To give you
a heads-up before I come in. To make sure it's something you
can do.'

The woman, Stephanie, said, 'Sure, sure.'

'I have to fly to New Guinea in early January. Then I need to
make a connecting flight to East New Britain. Then I have to make
a flight to Goroka, which is in the Highlands. I need you to arrange
for an armed guard to drive me up the mountain, up the Highlands
Highway from Goroka, so I can release my husband's ashes.'

'Wow,' was all she was capable of saying. Then, 'this is going to
be a challenge, but I'm sure I can help you. What if I make some

calls this arvo and you come in tomorrow and we can talk a little bit more about it?'

'Thank you.'

Di dropped round that night on her way home from work. If our schedules made it difficult for us to catch up for lunch during the week, she would buy a cheap vindaloo or a chicken tikka. I provided the gin. Neither of us, these days, had a lot of money to spare.

'Oh God, the fire is divine,' she said, collapsing onto one of the blue sofas, folding her legs beneath her. I grinned and slid a drink in front of her.

'LSD against the world 4 eva.' We clinked our glasses together.

Di chatted easily about her new job. Told me about plans she'd made to go away with her new man, Martin, and spend a blissful week in the south of New South Wales. Then she paused, gazed thoughtfully across the room at the photo on the wall of Wayne and me in Spain and cast me a soft, curious look.

'Aren't you afraid of what you're going to find out?'

Immediately I understood. Shook my head, met her eyes.

'Knowing the whole truth is better than not knowing, or only knowing bits about what supposedly happened. So much about the way he was makes sense to me now. You know, why he always looked uncomfortable when I started one of my rants about appreciating the past. So, I need to know a fuller version of the story.' I sat forward.

'Him doing what they claimed he did . . . that wasn't the man I knew.' I sighed. Frowned.

'Alternatively, maybe part of me has this absolutely hopeless romantic notion that I can prove he didn't do it?' I put my glass down on the coffee table and picked up a framed photo from our wedding day, showing me hugged within his arms, both of us smiling shyly. His whole body was curled around mine.

'That is the most beautiful I ever saw you,' Di said, taking the photo out of my hands and studying it. I picked my drink up again. Concentrated on stirring the lime around the glass with one finger.

'You know, the two of you together reminded me of *Beauty and the Beast.*'

Intrigued, I glanced up from my drink and laughed, sucking the fruit off my finger.

'Noooo. How can you think that?'

'Well, now we know what happened, what happened in 1978 . . .' she trailed off.

I held her eyes. 'It's okay. Tell me what you think.'

'He was so big, to start with. Especially when he would stand beside you back then. When I look at photos of you with him, it was like David said. He towered over you. So, the difference in your sizes is the initial thing that makes me think of the fairytale.'

Di's head was tilted to one side. She was speaking with her eyes fixed on the photo she held. 'But it's more . . . It's like he had some kind of rage inside. Anger he tried to control, but in the past just couldn't. Maybe from the way his father abused him? Is that why the night in Goroka happened? All that male rage?' She laid the photo face up on the table between us.

'His past must have been consuming him his whole life. I think he was such a vulnerable man, Suz. Vulnerable to his fear. Vulnerable about what he'd experienced at the hands of his father. Vulnerable to people finding out what happened back then. About *you* finding out. Except when you were around, I think you calmed him down. You were his quietness. His love. You offered him, finally, a kind of peaceful place to be.

'But now—well, now there is this twist we know about—you loved him for his strength, for the protection he offered you, for the arms he held you with. He needed someone to be kind to him. To love him for himself.'

The mellow light from the lamp shone down around my best friend. She leaned forward and placed the frame back in its place on the table.

'I know what you're saying,' I said. 'I understand. I think I did provide him with a safe place—for a while. But in the last month, something changed. He wasn't himself. I saw more of the beast you're talking about.'

'But like you've explained before, he must have been feeling very unwell. He wasn't himself.'

'When we were in Porto, three or four days before he died, he behaved very strangely. We'd stepped into a tapas place . . .' I paused, thinking hard, trying to get it right. 'I stopped near the bar. Smiled to the waiter. But Wayne just kept walking, like a blind man, through the main section of the place and out into the kitchen behind. It was so weird. I had to follow him and lead him back. The waiters gave us some very odd looks.'

'And something else had happened one night, before we left for that final trip. A few days before we left Granada.'

Di watched me carefully. Her expression was sympathetic. I sighed, took a gulp of the gin. And I told her.

One night we were in the square. At our favourite restaurant. It was late afternoon and the city was airless. He was sprawled in a chair. We'd both had way too much to drink and the tapas were insubstantial. The summer was fast approaching and tourists were already appearing from behind every building. It had been hot and muggy all afternoon.

We began arguing about Islam. He'd been speaking to me at length during that day about his memories from the Sydney siege. He'd been in

179

the city around the date it happened. The Charlie Hebdo shooting in Paris had kicked off a few days after we'd flown into Madrid. And then there'd also been the Bardo attack in Tunis—and we'd been making plans, of course, about flying down to Tunisia. It felt to both of us like we were travelling at a time when European history was changing and we had this terrible, but unique, front row seat to it all. So, he was trying to convince me that things could not work between people who practised Islam and ordinary modern-day Australians. I remember he said that, 'It's a religion from the Middle Ages. Past and present do not mix!'

I wasn't having it, of course. It was the first time, ever, I'd openly disagreed with him on anything serious, especially in public. I knew many practising Muslims who did not believe in such things, I shouted. What you describe is not what they believe. That is extremist thinking.

Before I knew it, he'd leapt up. His eyes like slits, he was shoving back his chair. He threw me the most enraged glance. His face was a dull brick red. Then he turned his back on me and stalked off into the night.

It was the most terrible, terrible night. He'd left me alone at the table, tears pouring down my cheeks because of his fury, his sudden disappearance, his blind beliefs. Glancing to the people on my right and then on my left, I tried to pretend nothing had happened. I tried to explain to our favourite waiter where 'John Wayne' had gone, flapping my arms about because my Spanish had disappeared.

He didn't come back. He stayed away all night. Didn't answer my text messages.

In the morning, after he finally returned, I cried. I was afraid he was going to leave me. I just didn't understand.

But recently, I remembered something he'd said to me that morning. After he came home.

I have to tell you something important, Suz, he'd said. We need to talk. Then he stopped. Like he was thinking about how to say it. Now isn't the time to talk about it. We'll talk about it later.

Di studied her empty glass. Sighed. 'I know what you're going to say.'

I leaned towards her. 'That night in the square reminded him of his fight with Caroline. In certain ways it was similar. They were arguing. Both of them were drunk. There was a scene. So, I think he left me that night in Granada because I reminded him too much of her and what he'd done. And he was afraid. Because maybe for the first time in his life the violence of the past and the present connected. And his mask started to slip.

'Then he died before he had time to tell me the truth.'

31

Mayfield, August 2017

ONE THING I FOUND DIFFICULT to manage, living on my own, was repairing stuff. I knew I could always attend classes at Bunnings, buy a drill, learn about hammers and tools and tape measures. As a second-wave feminist who'd cut my teeth on *The Women's Room*, I knew that it was my job not to stereotype by gender. But I also knew myself. So, because my brother had started his working life as an electrician, I asked him to help me with tasks like changing the light fittings, as I renovated my house.

And it was while he was up a stepladder putting in a new light, and I had my face tilted upwards watching him, that we began a conversation about Wayne's appeal trial. My brother also knew about that sort of stuff, as after his apprenticeship he had trained to become a police officer and had worked as a prosecutor. And emotionally, it felt safer not being face-to-face. My brother always told the truth. That might be a little confronting right now.

'Hey sis, I read the appeal yesterday, like you asked. What are you concerned about?' He was unscrewing the light fixture, intent on the job.

'Hang on. Just let me go get the printouts. I want to be able to quote you stuff.' And I raced down the hallway to my office, anxious to be able to discuss the appeal accurately.

I laid the pages on the kitchen bench. Chewed my lip.

'Not concerns so much . . . I guess. More to know what your impression was? The appeal trial occurred a few months after they convicted him. But for me, there seem to be unanswered questions on both sides. Do you agree?' I turned the pages carefully. 'I mean this, for example. From the doctor.'

And I read aloud.

I indicated to him that the deceased was dead. The defendant was extremely upset and tearful, very emotional . . . I stated 'What have you been doing here?' Subsequently, I examined the deceased. The defendant was emotional. I said in effect, 'How did it happen?' My memory is hazy here. The defendant said 'It doesn't matter how she was killed, I killed her'. It was a very emotional scene. I took the conciliatory role of suggesting maybe she died of a ruptured spleen, as her external injuries were slight . . .

'Then the appeal judge argues,' I said, summarising what had been reported, 'that if the injuries occurred because she fell down the stairs, or perhaps after cardiac massage had been applied too forcefully, which is what Wayne's defence counsel argued, there should have been some mention of this, rather than Wayne just saying he killed her. The judge also brings up the point that Wayne's flatmates were not called to give evidence by the defence. If they saw what happened, why not get them to say it?'

Pete frowned. Chucked me down some screws.

'We don't need those anymore.'

I stuffed the screws into the pocket of my jeans.

'When Wayne died in Portugal, and the doctors and police all arrived, I couldn't *stop* explaining about what had happened and what I did to try and save him. I know how it feels, when someone you love dies in front of you. I went over and over it with the police and the ambulance officers, longing for my account to provide answers. But the doctor in Goroka that night maintained everyone remained silent, except Wayne. Who said he'd killed her and it didn't matter how.'

Pete asked me to pass him the pliers.

'And I think Constable Atu's evidence is highly questionable. Don't you think that too? Even one of the appeal judges says it doesn't add up. Atu was the only one who claimed he saw ...' I swallowed ... I could do this. I *could* say this. 'He is the only one who claims he saw Wayne stomping on her at the bottom of the stairs.'

Martha had never mentioned this horrendous piece of evidence. So, when I first read it in the appeal notes, it hit me viscerally. Like a violent punch to the belly. I felt so nauseous, I ran to the bathroom because I thought I was about to vomit. It was one thing to believe my husband had killed a young woman accidentally. Though that was challenging enough. But that he had killed her deliberately? So viciously? So callously? The idea made me shudder like I was ill with a fever. It was a mixture of disgust and fear. I had trusted Wayne so implicitly. We had been so intimate. I had given everything I was to him. Given everything up for him. Had I married a stranger? Someone I never really knew at all? A monster? I had cried like I hadn't cried in months. Great ragged sobs. I cried like the day of his memorial service.

With my heart in my mouth, because I wanted to believe in Wayne, I said, 'What I don't understand is, if there were so many people watching, why did no one else report it?'

I flicked through the pages till I found the right spot. Read aloud again.

He was awakened by the deceased, who hit at him with a slat from the veranda gate. She was, on all accounts, quite hysterical. She obviously bore the appellant a grudge. Probably because she was considerably affected by liquor, she was irritated he had spent the day on his own, and not with her, not that this was his fault.

After much confusion, the couple ended up outside after she had thrown stones at the flat's building and drawn a crowd of spectators to the scene by her demented behaviour. Ultimately a police patrol car drew up and the critical events of the night commence about this time.

Pete said, 'Atu's evidence was considered believable because of one crucial factor—he made a statement only hours after the incident—supporting his version of the story. This accords with evidence law and case law as what is considered credible—not information that has been provided at a later date.

'In contrast, Wayne made what appear to be admissions to the doctor very shortly after the incident, but unlike the police officer, he refused to say anything until interviewed the next day, and only bringing in the defence of her falling down the stairs once at court. A strong inference can be drawn that this defence was a concoction after the event, because nothing was revealed to the doctor at the scene, to the police at the scene or when he was interviewed.'

I fiddled with the papers on the benchtop, tidied them up, shuffled them together. Thwack.

'Yep. I understand.' Still finding it hard to physically say the words, I stuttered. 'S . . . so, in a rage . . . he stomped on her? Like Constable Atu said? Stomped on her at the bottom of the stairs? That's why she died? I just can't imagine the man I knew doing that, Pete.'

185

I started reading aloud again.

The State case, largely supported by only one witness, Constable Atu . . . is that the deceased was observed by Atu to be lying on the concrete below the steps, and Atu says the appellant was 'stomping' with his leg bent at the knee, bringing it down . . . Mr Griffin of counsel for the appellant certainly does not accept this, he says it was dark . . . Atu had no time to make these observations . . . is a pretty worthless witness.

'Remember, sis, the final decision was manslaughter, because they believed the crime not to be premeditated . . . But I agree with you. Defence should have called the other occupants of the house.'

I bent over the bench, searched for what I was looking for. Read through it quickly, finger trailing beneath the dense sentences. Looked up at Pete.

'Even the doctor reported he found no significant marks on her body. Had Wayne kicked her, like they said, surely the bruising would have shown? And the bit about him, the same doctor, being allowed to conduct the post mortem on the deceased's body, "through some official irregularity or misunderstanding". What was that about?'

Pete said, 'The case was certainly not conducted properly. Not the way I understand it. Interesting to note one of the appeal judges did comment he may not have agreed with the trial judge on some things but could not find any grounds to support the appeal. No grounds, and no real evidence to negate Constable Atu.'

I continued to read and to summarise simultaneously.

'Wayne denied the stomping. He says he managed to get her up to the top level of the staircase but that at the door she broke away. Fell down the flight of stairs. They all agree that if that's correct, it's a strong defence for him.'

I quoted again.

This raises a strong defence indeed, for the deceased died not long thereafter, within the flat, from what, in lay terms, could be described as a ruptured heart. The medical evidence, differing as it does in some respects, supports the proposition that a strong blow to the chest could have caused the rupture, which inevitably led to a quick death, as the tear caused by the rupture was not insignificant. Thus, a nasty fall down this flight of stairs could raise a very reasonable doubt as to the cause of death or establish it . . . but His Honour found that this injury occurred from the 'stomping' at the foot of the stairs.

Pete mumbled through the screwdriver he held between his teeth and I passed up a new light globe. Then he said, very clearly, as he laid the light globe on the top step of the ladder, 'Wayne killed Caroline Benny, sis. Albeit, accidentally. But there is also the statement that he slapped her face, in front of the crowd. He admitted to that. Domestic violence, alcohol, always a potent mix. You can't gloss over that, even though I know how much you'd like to.'

Reading the appeal notes, discussing the case with people I trusted, didn't help me understand what had happened to Caroline that night. But it did make me realise why Wayne perceived the past to be the enemy, and how he'd been hiding during the years he'd been working in Mt Isa and Kalgoorlie—working down a mine shaft in the dark, in the middle of the Australian desert. All those times he'd insisted we live in the moment? Now it made perfect sense.

32

Mayfield, August 2017

BUT PLANS TO UNCOVER THE real story had to be put on hold. Because in the few remaining days of August, early on a Monday morning, the buzzing of my phone startled me from sleep. Squinting through the dimness, struggling to release myself from the blankets, from my dreams about the Highlands, I'd fumbled around, feeling for the bedside table. Snatched up the phone.

'Susan? It's Paul, from the Gardenia Ward, at Forest Lodge.' His voice was sharp in the silence of my bedroom.

'Carol has deteriorated very suddenly. I'm very concerned. Her breathing patterns have altered dramatically. She's running a temp and she's vomited several times. I think we need to call in the palliative care team.'

Shocked. And not shocked. The beat of a bird's wing.

'Right, Paul. Right. I'll call my brother. We'll be over straight away.'

I hung up and punched in the number.

'Pete, Pete?' And my voice cracked finely like a porcelain vase. 'The RN just rang from Mum's. We need to get over there.'

He and Jan, he yelled, would get straight in the car. 'We'll be right over to yours. We'll all go together.'

I listed things in my head while I dressed, sitting on the side of my bed with the light off, dragging on my jeans: *text Jonno, cancel today's classes, make my bed. Where the fuck are my keys?*

Mum rested so slightly between the white sheets, as flat as an undercooked pancake. One eye was open. The little pinprick of light that had been there yesterday when I'd visited had vanished. This staring eye was dull, cloudy yellow. A single dried string of mucus lay across it. Her chest was a square frame, heaving up, then levelling out with a gasp. Pete fell to his knees beside her bed. His face cheek-to-cheek against hers.

'Oh, Mum.'

Jan backed up in the doorway, her hands cradled over her mouth.

'We think her lethargic state is caused by an infection in the cancer on the back of her neck,' said Paul.

I nodded. Pete nodded. This was the cancer we couldn't approve to have removed, because Mum wouldn't have survived the anaesthetic. Or the transition into the outside world; to an unfamiliar, noisy, hospital.

Shifting silently to the opposite side of the room from Pete, I sat gingerly beside Mum on her bed. It already felt as though stillness and quiet were critical for her.

'The antibiotics we're giving her are making her sick. The doctor has ordered that all her medication be ceased.' Eyes tracing my mother's face, I squeezed her limp hand.

'We're here, Mum. Pete and Jan and me. It's all right.'

Paul said, 'When the palliative care nurse comes in, I'll let you know. We'll ring the doctor, but I don't know if he'll be in today.'

Jan left to get ready for work. Then Pete and I settled into two of the chairs in the room. We remained in them, like sentries, on either side of our mother. Other than when we slept, or when I raced home to maintain my timetabled classes, or Pete staggered to the gym—we sat there.

My brother and I shared one mind in terms of what we wanted for Mum. No unnecessary suffering, but no invasive intervention either. A tranquil space and some kind of dignity. What was termed 'a good death'. Because, God knows, she deserved it. But it wasn't quite what she received, even though we tried our best.

The doctor arrived at three in the afternoon of the following day, and prescribed morphine as necessary.

'How long?' Pete ventured.

'Two or three days, at most.'

A palliative nurse called in from the large hospital close by, ventured into our room, respectful and cautious. 'Hello, family,' and 'it might not be end-of-life today, but it will not be long.'

Then Mum stopped swallowing any food or fluid.

At the nursing home, my brother and I sat still, in some kind of suffocating tableau—a cracked, European oil painting with a dull patina. Formal and stiff, we sat. Hour upon hour, watching her suffer. Watching her die.

One night, after Peter left to go home, I sat beside my mother for a little longer. The nursing home was quiet now. It was after 9 p.m. There was a small lamp lit beside Mum's bed and she was calmer.

I started thinking about my childhood and everything my mother had done for me.

Both my parents had been good people. Both from the working classes. I remember them working hard every day, using their initiative as a means to 'get ahead'. Remnants of family existed for both of them, but in reality, they were alone. From nothing, they made a family of their own.

They concentrated on raising themselves into the middle class, to better provide for their two most-thanked-for children. It was the neat and healthy Carol, in the black-and-white photographs taken during the early years of her marriage, who was responsible for raising me. Duty motivated my young mother. She wanted to be the best wife and mother she could be. Married at eighteen, and ten years her husband's junior, her diligence shone across her freshly scrubbed face. Her bag always matched her shoes. She always had her short fringe arranged neatly across her forehead. Cleanliness was more important than godliness.

As a young girl, my mother had been required to look after things in her own home from a very young age. From about eight years of age. The cooking and cleaning were not done unless she managed it in and around going to school. This aspect of her character was simple enough to understand if you knew the back story—my grandmother had been left unhinged, as Mum referred to it, after losing her only son to meningitis. Barry, my mother's only brother, had been five years old.

Mum was only a child when her brother died. But it was Beryl, my grandmother, who never recovered. I remember her as a wizened old stick of a thing, with a sweep of white hair; crippled with arthritis, hunched over the form guide, calculating her bets, cramming peanut butter and SAOs into her mouth.

Self-control and keeping a tidy house were things my mother learnt to value about herself. It wasn't till after my dad died that I remember my mum finally relaxing enough to enjoy life. After Dad died, Mum started travelling. She travelled all over the world. And we finally stepped out of the roles of mother and daughter and became friends. It was the worst of ironies that she became sick with Alzheimer's disease at the age of sixty-seven.

John, my father, was less scrupulous. Where my mother would allow herself one shandy, if pushed, my dad was more likely to drink too much beer on a daily basis, laughing and making what are now known as politically incorrect statements. Looking back, I think he was probably a functioning alcoholic.

I remember, as a child, sitting grumpy and tired in my damp swimmers, on a beach towel in the station wagon with my brother beside me and my mother sitting demurely in the front seat. All of us were drinking the lemon squash bought and passed through the open window to us by my father. He remained drinking inside the pub for most of the afternoon, while the wet sand on my skin dried to dust.

Dad kept a hammer under the front seat of the taxi he drove, for when it was dole day, he said, and he would get jobs from the housing commission area. According to my father, the unemployed were rich for just one day a fortnight. The hammer was for those days. Just in case, he said. I never doubted he would use it.

Unfortunately, for everyone, Dad had an affair when I was three, just before Pete was adopted. *Dull Hull,* the name they had called my father at school, certainly no longer applied. He was dull no longer. She had big breasts and was a slovenly red head, according to my mum, who relayed all this to me many years later, after Dad had finally succumbed to his second bout of cancer. The radical radiotherapy, employed in the 1950s for his first bout, had been responsible for his infertility.

After four months away with the slovenly one, my father was permitted to return home, because as Mum said, what choice did she have? No such thing as a single mother's pension existed back in 1964. And her own mother was in no fit state to look after the only grandchild. Mum didn't want to have to farm me out around the neighbourhood while she went back to work. Was that a fit upbringing for a child who had been adopted?

Furthermore, she was terrified the government could somehow take her baby, if they discovered her situation as a woman without support. For this reason, my parents' marriage continued—because of me! And to *get* Pete (Pete was to be adopted in the 'proper' way), Mum had to suffer the indignity of state welfare officers visiting the house on a monthly basis to ensure the family had returned to normal after my dad's mistake. Mum never, *ever*, forgave my father.

Two iconic images of my parents remained with me—from the time I was about twelve. The old stereo was playing the 33s which both of them loved. Music was played often in our house. Their tastes were eclectic, formed from instinct, not education. They listened to everything that moved them, from the Boston Pops playing the classics, to Robeson and 'Ol' Man River'.

This particular morning Mum was singing along with the Engelbert Humperdinck song 'Please Release Me (Let Me Go)'.

With a red gingham apron fastened about her neat waist, she was in the kitchen, washing out the Vegemite jars, later to be used as cordial glasses. The kitchen wallpaper, chosen with my mother's impeccable taste, circa 1974, was a vivid geometric pattern of lime green.

There she was, the perfect housewife, thrifty and tidy, crooning to an empty house about the unhappiness her marriage was causing her. I'm not sure if this sad irony was lost on my mum or not. But it was not lost on me, even at that young age. It probably accounted for the upside-down wedding photograph, slapped away on the bedside table next to where I now sat.

In contrast, my father: grubby, terry-towelling hat pulled unattractively down around his ears, half-pissed, cooking the Sunday night barbecue, swatting mosquitoes at dusk amongst the overgrown blackberry bushes down in the wilds of the back yard. Empty beer cans form a crooked pyramid on a dinner plate, pooling with the congealed blood from sausages that have sat out too long. Randomly, he would chuck scraps of meat to the magpies he enticed into the garden. He loved birds. I feed the magpies now, too. In my own back garden.

I'd read my first poem to my father, too.

It was my dad who had told me to go looking for my parents. Just before he'd died. Because he was illegitimate and had never been told who his own father was.

Reflecting on my childhood, sitting beside Mum's bed, forced me to think about my genetic parents again. And finally, I was able to put them into clear perspective.

When I'd left the Durty Nelly in Perth, I'd been thankful to get away. I didn't want to think about either one of them anymore, or have anything more to do with them. I'd turned my focus completely to Wayne and our Granada adventure.

Soon, though, both my adoptive parents would be dead. While in a surreal set of circumstances, both my natural parents would be alive. The realisation placed my mum and dad in sharp relief against Enid and O'Connor. Thank God, I thought to myself, driving away from the nursing home, that I'd been adopted. Strained as our house had been. And as much as I'd never fitted in. Otherwise, what might my life have been like? My dad had gifted me some of his smart-arsery and his love of reading. He encouraged me to follow an unconventional path. 'Never be a sheep, Susan,' he would say. My mum had passed on her determination. Her love for travel. I felt endless gratitude.

The vigil continued. At unexpected times throughout the day—my feet propped on the unforgiving frame of the bed, attempting to read, but unable to resist raising my face each time Mum whimpered—a nursing assistant from some other ward would knock, peek around the door, sidle in. By now everyone understood we wanted quiet. There'd be another shake of another head.

'How can she keep going? How many days has it been now?'

It had been ten days. Long hours of nothing. I could still smell the odour on my clothes when I returned home each night, when I'd drag my shirt to my nose and sniff, thinking I was imagining it. But the stench of death had attached itself to me.

We called in all the kids. Jonno drove up from Sydney, sat beside his grandma, hunched over, shoulders hiding the tears. I left the room so he could say goodbye.

Twelve days.

'Is she really dying?' I whispered to Pete.

The nurses entered to reposition Mum. Interrupted their own chatter halfway through the door. Pete and I stood up, stretched, getting ready to leave.

'Bridie from H ward has just passed away. She went for seventeen days,' said the little nurse with dirty-blonde hair and a ring through her nose, as she stacked fresh sheets and pillowcases on the chair I'd just vacated.

'What do we need to be looking for?' Pete asked.

And they repeated what we'd been told a thousand times.

'Cold feet and hands. Blue fingernails. Long breaks between taking a breath. The gurgling sound of Cheyne–Stoke breathing.'

But none of this happened.

Apparently, the nurses had been holding a backroom sweep on who would 'go' first, Bridie or Mum. Pete and I both found this amusing, which probably spoke for our frame of mind.

On day thirteen, Pete decided to stay the night on a mattress on the floor, beside Mum's bed.

He texted me at 10 p.m.

'I'm not going home. Paul is concerned her breathing patterns have changed again.'

'Do you want me to come in?'

'No, you've got to be here in the morning. It's okay.'

We'd both been warned 'it's close' so many times, I didn't really think twice about it.

The phone rang again at four in the morning.

33

Mayfield, November 2017

SIX WEEKS LATER, AFTER THE funeral, my bestie and I lay slumped across the blue couches in my lounge room. We were listening to James Taylor. A hot, dry early start to summer meant I had the front door propped open to allow a southerly breeze to drift down the hallway.

'We've been grieving for Mum for ten years. Can you believe it?' I stared at the floor.

'Do you think she knew what was going on?'

'Sometimes, maybe a year or two ago, even though she couldn't speak—I did wonder. But God, I have no idea, really. Food, maybe. A warm hand holding hers. The sun on her face. I think that's what it boiled down to in the end.'

'To be honest, really honest,' I scrunched up my face because I knew it was an awful thing to say, 'compared to Wayne dying, Mum's death has touched me to a lesser degree. I don't know if it's because I'm still grieving so hard for Wayne. Perhaps Mum has been caught in the backwash of my mourning for him? Or is it because we've been inching towards her passing away, day by day, for such a long time? Anticipatory grief they call it. Because we knew she was going to die eventually from Alzheimer's, the grief has been running like a dripping tap all these years.

'I feel saddened, humbled, and actually angry about the *manner* of Mum's death. That she had to suffer those two weeks without food or water. But not shattered. It's strange how the more deaths you experience, the more you understand that the sorrow you feel is different for each person. Wayne's death still has the ability to fell me.'

My best friend spoke hesitantly.

'And you still feel this way, even after everything you've found out since?'

'It seems to me,' I paused, and breathed out wearily, 'that there are two versions of the story about what happened in Goroka. Both of them violent.' I twisted my hands together, round and round. I could hear the dry rasp of skin.

'I think . . . that either the police officer and the original judge are right, and Wayne meant to kill her,' I swallowed, eyes on my hands, 'or he pushed her away and she fell. And he couldn't reach her in time.'

My best friend contemplated her drink. 'And what about the parallel between him and your father?'

I looked up.

'What?'

'There's a parallel between Wayne and your natural father. Both of them were hiding their pasts, perhaps unable to face up to whatever they'd done, certainly unable to talk about it. Both were trying to pretend the past didn't exist and carrying those secrets around with them. Both of them were using different names. Your father drove all around Australia trying to escape his history. In a way, I feel that's what Wayne did when he was travelling around Europe with you. Just running from his past. There were two different versions of how you were born. And there are two different versions of how Caroline died in New Guinea.'

'I've never thought about it that way.'

Di spoke quietly. 'Just follow your plans, amigo. Talk to John. He is the person who will know what truly happened. I also think it's a good idea that you only ever plan on going to New Guinea once.' She leaned back. 'You weren't sitting with us at your mum's wake when everyone started talking ...'

And she told me about how unhappy everyone was about me going. Jonno and Caitlin being the loudest objectors. How the idea of me being alone was what concerned them the most.

It also concerned me. So, in an effort to be practical I'd accepted an offer from Martha's second husband, Robert, who still lived in Moresby, to meet me and help me when I arrived there. And after watching a video that had just hit the news about an Australian family driving west of Port Moresby who'd been ambushed by the 'rascal boys' up a mountain road, I was relieved I'd arranged for a private security guard to accompany me up to the Daulo Pass in the Highlands where I planned to release Wayne's ashes. The video had scared me. The kids in the back seat were screaming. The father reversed at high speed up a winding clifftop road while four men raced towards them from the car pulled across the road in front. The rascals who poured out of the first car held machetes and a rifle.

34

Newcastle, November 2017

Before I left for New Guinea, Mum's house had to be cleaned one final time. Pete and Jan were upstairs in the kitchen, Jonno and Caitlin around the back in the garden, bickering over who was going to use the whipper snipper. Ashleigh and her dad puttered about in the spare bedroom. Meanwhile, downstairs, Di and I were sorting through the linen press in the laundry.

My mother's housekeeping had always seemed to possess a sense of mythical vigour. But in the years before she'd moved to the nursing home, the Alzheimer's had distorted that aspect of her identity. The house was now a senseless jumble: saucepans stuck inside other saucepans, with handles loose or missing, which all would crash to the floor when anybody opened the kitchen cabinets; burnt-out frypans, discarded in the far corners under the laundry sink; dozens of empty light globe boxes, stacked in uneven towers inside the linen press.

'How old do you think these towels are?' Di dragged piles of them, thin and wrinkled, from the back of the cupboard. She was balanced on the top of the stepladder, handing everything down to me.

I stuck my nose into the rough material and made a face. 'God knows.'

Shoving them into a bin bag, I glanced about the room. We'd already tied off six loads of ancient linen: cloth serviettes stained with spilt tea, striped flannelette sheets with rips the size of somebody's leg, tea towels crinkled with the dust of every one of the sixty years she'd wiped a dish.

'God, look at this!' Di heaved out a cardboard box, collapsing at the corners, and balanced it on one arm as she bent down to place it on top of Mum's old twin tub. Hundreds of black-and-white photographs, and colour images stained brown, the way they do from the developing procedures back in the 1970s, spilled out over the edges. We stood side-by-side for about an hour, in my mother's laundry, my best friend and I, selecting pictures from our shared past: the three of us wearing neatly pressed, new school uniforms on the first day of Year 7; Liz's wedding, her face shining with happiness; a birthday party for Jonno, here in Mum's back yard, our kids grappling over each other to ride his new bike.

'My God, amigo, look at these! Fifty years at least of brilliant memories.'

And then, I recall, I squatted down on the cold tiles, my back propped against the wall, because a wave of understanding had washed over me.

'What?' Di asked, kneeling down in front of me. Her face close to mine. And I pointed to the pictures.

'It's going to sound dreadful.'

'What?' she repeated, grabbing my hand.

I swallowed, and my mouth was so dry my lips were stuck together. I tried again.

'I had a life, didn't I? A whole life, I mean, before I met Wayne.'

She waited.

'That life was full of people, celebrations, love. Wonderful things happened. I had a life before I met him. And somehow, I forgot about all that . . .'

The next bit I whispered.

'Looking at these photos reminds me I can have a life again.'

Later, after everyone had gone home, I sat on Mum's balcony. The view of Newcastle was laid out before me; I could see all the way to the Pacific Ocean.

Moving on was so difficult. It was such a fine balance between remembering Wayne and claiming back a life for myself. One minute I became enthusiastic about what I could achieve, then in the next instant I felt dishonourable to Wayne. I couldn't live in the past, but I couldn't forget about it either. Seeing those photos reminded me that both the past and the present are equally important to who we are and the way we live our life.

I realised that Wayne's death had allowed me to finally strengthen my own sense of identity. Portugal and afterwards, at the little house in Morpeth, the trip to New Guinea—all these experiences, both terrible and restorative, meant I was evolving, even in my mid-fifties, and in a more profound way than I ever expected when I started the search for Enid and her Irishman.

Wayne had lost his life. Mum was dead. Liz was dead. Dad was dead. My mother, my father, my best friend and my husband. But I had made it home from Spain. And I was about to fly to the Highlands. Whatever number of sisters I may have called Susan, or how many fathers claimed me, or the level of love I held for my husband—none amounted to the whole of me.

Wayne and I had loved the Aristophanes story about soulmates happily cartwheeling around the world. We believed it symbolised how we felt about each other. But now? Perhaps the story represented the importance of connecting your past with your present—and it was that link that made us absolute. Connecting both the positive aspects of yourself to the difficult ones. Accepting that what has gone before is the prologue for who you are in the present.

Aristophanes' story is not about searching for a soulmate. It's about embracing our entire selves.

I continued to sit on my mum's balcony, watching the dusk settle in. And at long last, a great calmness wrapped itself about me. The magpies sang to each other and I smiled.

35

Mayfield, late November 2017

THE TRIP WAS ALMOST UPON me, when Silas texted.

> Hi Aunty Sue
>
> I heard a rumour you're heading up to PNG. I think that's
> awesome! I'm heading up this Christmas as well and we
> could catch up somewhere along the way if you like.
>   I'd be more than happy to show you around Rabaul
> and East New Britain too. And if you're up to it, a visit
> with my dad. Just ideas though. Your adventure is
> yours and I don't want to take that away from you.

There was no need to think about what Silas was suggesting. Gorgeous-looking boy that he was, half Papuan and mad for football, just like his uncle; I immediately sent him the details about my trip, including dates and flights. Then added, almost as an afterthought: 'Kind of a sensitive question, but do you think your dad would want a small amount of Wayne's ashes?'

204

About the ashes . . . I think he would . . . I actually
do . . . but we should talk before you come home. Don't
worry we are expecting you now and want to make sure
you're ok . . . when we talk, I'll want to know who your
guard is and who is looking after you . . . this is not a
stab at your intelligence I'm just looking out . . . I do not
want you to get taken advantage of . . . talk soon.

In those words, I heard the echo of my Wayne. It was his knowledge on offer. His security and strength by my side, guiding me towards John.

Meeting this six-foot-four brother of the man I loved both intrigued me and dismayed me. Even Martha had not seen John since his early twenties—now he was close to sixty. Wayne had first spoken to me in 2014 about his years of hankering to get John to Australia, and his confusion about how it could possibly work. I now believed it was John's reluctance to leave New Guinea and the fact that Wayne had been deported to Australia and was not allowed to return to the country he loved that had conspired to keep the brothers apart.

It had been a winter weekend in the central west of New South Wales in 2014, and Wayne and I had rugged up for a stroll along the walking track beside the slow, low, meandering Macquarie River. During summer, Dubbo broiled. But in June and July the temperature often fell below freezing. Frosted tufts of grass sparkled like a European Christmas.

I have a photograph some stranger took of us that afternoon. Both of us wearing our sunglasses against the sunlight filtering between the arms of the white gums. I wore my duffle coat and scarf, Wayne stood tall beside me, wearing a checked shirt the colour of apples. Our faces are lit up by love and the winter sun.

'I've had an email from Tammi,' he started, halting by a bench seat and tugging me down beside him.

I sat forward on the seat and half turned to face him, waiting for him to speak. The river lay before us. A spreading willow rested behind us. Even though we'd only been together for a couple of years, I believed I understood the sacred nature of the relationship he had with his brother.

Tammi, John's ex-wife, lived closer to Rabaul, with access to the internet, and was the only regular form of communication between the two men. She would send emails to Wayne every so often, keeping him informed of how John was doing. But even she found John difficult to predict. For John was notoriously, famously, reclusive. Had 'gone troppo'. Wild. Living off the grid in the jungle. The snatches of information Wayne let fall riveted me. There was, for example, the story of the brutal murder involving two of John's workers several years ago. It had cost John $40,000 in reparation payments—which he did not have. Wayne had paid for most of it through a bank account Tammi had set up.

'John is getting older. Living up in the mountains isn't what it used to be. I can pay the fares, get him down to New South Wales, but I don't know what it's going to be like for him. I never have figured out how he could adapt to living in Australia. With us going to Spain next year, I don't know if it's a good idea anymore.' He tiredly rubbed his face with both hands.

We both sat silent for a while. He absently stroked my hair. I watched a small, thin boy, standing alone on the bank of the river, repeatedly throw a stick for his tatty-eared dog.

'If I could have a wish, Suz, it would be for you to meet John. To see us standing side-by-side. The man each of us might have become under other circumstances. I would like to hear your thoughts after that meeting—on what you would perceive.'

He squeezed me closer, one massive arm wrapped around me.

Now I would partially make Wayne's wish come true. I would meet John, because he no longer could.

I wondered about so many things. How much would John remind me of Wayne? And how would that make me feel? Emotion was pooling inside me already.

I wanted to meet John, and in another way I didn't.

For a while now, I had felt guilty writing about Wayne. But I also wanted to share his struggles and his strengths with others. In part, I felt I was paying homage to him, despite the dreadful things revealed. How could I write about the importance of truth and not tell the whole truth myself? But how might John feel about it?

Lastly, I thought about something I'd heard other people discuss: imagine that somehow, someone gives you five minutes to talk again with the person you love who has passed away. What would I ask Wayne? Or would I just tell him how much I still love him?

I felt that talking to John was going to be a little like that. It was the closest I could come to spending one last time with the man I loved so much.

No one remembered Wayne the way I did. Many of my friends in Newcastle had never even met him. There was no one to talk about him with. Di and I kept Liz alive and close in our hearts by constantly referencing her in our conversations. But I had no one to do that with for Wayne. We had spent so much time at my place, in Dubbo, before we left for Spain, and I'd never had a chance to know his friends very well. Sometimes in my mind it seemed that Granada was all a dream.

Talking to John, I would be talking to someone who reminded me of Wayne and who loved him as I did. I wanted these conversations very much. But I was frightened too; of what emotions might be unleashed.

I also wondered whether he would be able to tell me what really happened.

Five days before flying to Moresby
Apparently, people in Goroka had never forgotten the death of Caroline Benny. She had been a member of a loved and respected family, and the controversial case was still debated and discussed often. At the time, her death had been publicised far and wide within the country—due to my husband being white, due to Caroline being black, due to her family situation.

A suggestion was made that if certain men in Goroka discovered I was Wayne's wife, payback would follow. I was told, frankly, that being gang-raped would be the least of my punishment; the best I could hope for.

Claims were even made that the security officer I'd hired could not be completely trusted—this would depend on who he was and where his loyalties lay. Or the police. Or the airport guards. The insinuation was that any of these men could or would simply hand me over to men with machetes. If they found out who I was.

Four days before flying to Moresby
Steroids I swallowed in a last-ditch effort to calm my inflamed lungs, to drag my unwilling asthma back to manageability before the humidity of New Guinea, induced the worst case of herpes I'd ever suffered.

I raced to the doctor's again and added to my private PNG pharmacy pack. My usual GP was away, and the locum I saw was very young and very inexperienced. He prescribed an entire bottle of little white prednisone tablets, just in case the asthma flared again. He was nervous about me becoming trapped in the Highlands 'without the right drugs being available'. I halved the bottle and left at least twenty of those magic pills in my pantry, as I wasn't sure such a copious number of steroid tablets would go down well at PNG's border control.

For, in addition to the cartload of steroids in my pack, I carried Doxycycline for malaria, just in case, anti-nausea tablets for the plane journey to the Highlands and the winding Highlands Highway, and the big guns—the anti-viral horse sluggers, Valaciclovir, to calm the blisters on my bum.

Three days before flying to Moresby
I emailed an international private investigating firm in Port Moresby, asking them to research what had happened in Goroka in 1978. Caitlin had come back to me to tell me her inquiries here in Australia had come to nought. My search of the internet had also turned up nothing—other than the appeal verdict. I'd had the verdict for some time now, and was currently reading the judgement for the fifth time, still uncertain about the truth of that night. Still trying to understand what had happened.

But following grief, the mind and the heart, as I'd already leant, were not always in rhythm. Waiting for some kind of moral clarity to kick in, to guide me in how I was meant to feel, to react, to think, was an endless, fruitless preoccupation. Because this was the man I adored—whose face I would stare at with complete trust; whose life I valued more than my own. This was the man who'd shared with me some of the deepest joy I'd ever known; who'd defended me from the Romani man in Granada; crossed the Nullarbor Plain with me to help me face my father, and who'd chosen me to marry him, above any other woman. He'd given up his career and whisked me off to Spain. He'd taken the greatest amount of pleasure in caring for me and spoiling me. I didn't know what to believe. *He loved me and I didn't want to imagine he'd done this or I might lose my sense of place beside him*. So, I experienced conflicting thoughts about what Wayne had done. The tension was almost unbearable. As I tumbled the problem about in my head, no one idea, or emotion, would merge with the other.

Anger and resentment—yes. That I hadn't been told: that it had been kept a secret from me. Those ancient feelings from my adoption kicked me in the teeth again. Hadn't I a right to know that my husband had been in gaol for killing his partner? Either with intent or by accident? Shouldn't that secret have been shared with me? There was an underlying sense I'd been conned—lied to by a number of people; made a fool of, even. Many people were in on this conspiracy of silence and I was only just beginning to realise how many people knew, while the truth had been denied to me. Someone famous once said, love without truth is hypocrisy.

Dreadful sorrow for Wayne. That he'd had to live with the guilt, the burden of this act and this appalling secret, all his life. The consequences of one terrible, drunken, violent night had irredeemably changed the entire course of his life. Changed him. Changed his prospects, his future, his confidence and the relationships with his family and, most significantly, his relationship with himself. I imagine he never really fought his way free of the shame or of his conscience. Otherwise, I believe he would have told me.

Confusion and culpability. About raising the subject after all this time in the face of his family, who wanted it forgotten. About my responsibility to keep it a secret, for my husband's sake. About things I might have said differently when he was alive, if I'd known.

Forgiveness or condemnation. At what point do you move from blame to tolerance? At what point do you stop loving someone? Is violence explainable? And is it something I can pardon? The nuance around whether the crime had been committed by accident or committed intentionally complicated the struggle.

And Caroline? Where were my ire and sorrow for her? As the journey to Goroka shifted nearer, Caroline shifted closer too.

It was because I had started to think about what the word violence meant. What the difference between manslaughter and murder really was. What different forms of physical abuse against women existed. I started to read more widely about New Guinea. Changed my focus from what travellers to the country had said to various academic explanations accounting for the prevailing savagery against women.

It seemed reports of physical and sexual abuse were not exaggerated. In fact, all of the literature I examined stated that violence against women in PNG was grossly underreported.

It was within this atmosphere that Wayne had grown up. And there was, of course, his father who *beat him black-and-blue*. With the space reserved for a maternal figure vacant, I needed to examine the circumstances of Caroline's death with a clear eye.

According to every human rights paper I studied, the gendered violence in New Guinea is due to widespread poverty; legislation being written around gender inequality that is never enacted; customary traditional practices such as payback, a belief in sorcery, bride price and polygamy; lack of educational opportunity for girls; lack of access to birth control; the problems associated with a pluralist legal system (police would rather domestic abuse be handled by the family); government corruption; police corruption; widespread issues concerning the shift of power from colonial administration to independence.

I spent days searching for Caroline's name on Google. But there were no reports about her death. Caroline's murder had been kept away from the public gaze. In fact, there were no mentions of her name at all, except for the court documents and the one mention in a Trove article reporting the crime.

I wondered about her family. How they'd coped. I wondered about Wayne's family and their way of coping.

Was I doing something foolish? Something reprehensible?

Two days before flying to Moresby
I took a deep breath and contacted Keith Jackson AM, who managed a blog called PNG Attitude. His knowledge about PNG was vast, and many people contributed to his blog pages. He replied with some emails forwarded from a man named Arthur Smedley, who lived in Milne Bay where Caroline Benny was from.

> I remember the matter of Caroline Benny. I was working in Milne Bay at the time and it was a topic of conversation among station staff. She came from a well-known Milne Bay family.
>
> I also recall a discussion with some government lawyers during a Supreme Court visit to Alotau on circuit. It may have been with Clive Wall, but I'm not sure—anyway, the lawyer said the charges were reduced to manslaughter because it was an accidental death.
>
> Caroline's father was a builder who worked in Lae and the family was living there at the time.
>
> Another thing I recall is many people saying how sad it was, and they talked about her being a very beautiful girl/woman.
>
> Caroline's father died some years ago, but apparently her elderly mother is back living on the Trobriands. One of Caroline's brothers is also on the island. Caroline was the only girl in the family.
>
> Apparently, the family were/are a major land-owning clan and strong members of the United Church (Methodist

Church) community and some of their land, near the
government station of Losuia, was given to the Methodist
Church when it established on the Trobriands in the late
1800s. One of Caroline's grandfathers may have been a
Methodist pastor, trained by the Australian missionaries.

Caroline's mother's name is Lisila (Trobriand
pronunciation of Priscilla) and she is what they refer to as
the first *nunu*—the first or eldest daughter. As you know,
being a matrilineal society, women play a significant role,
with inheritance and clan coming from the mother. Being
the first *nunu*, Lisila is the eldest daughter of the eldest
daughter going back generations. A first *nunu* is also the
female head of the individual sub-clan.

As the first and only daughter, Caroline would have
become the first *nunu* following her mother's passing. With
Caroline's death that individual sub-clan could come to an
end, unless there are other relatives regarded as closely
enough related to take over clan leadership—but it would
not be directly inherited as happens in the normal manner.

Caroline's passing is something that even many younger
people know about today. They say her father was very
emotional about the matter for many years, possibly until his
death, and would often break down in tears if his daughter
was mentioned. After the accident the mother never spoke
of her daughter to outsiders, was very stoic and apparently
grieved privately.

The family never ever mentioned Caroline's name and
would not permit family members to use the name. Only
in the last year has a family member (a nephew) given
the name to a daughter—and only after discussions and
permission from the immediate family. Those I spoke to

mentioned what I said in the earlier email, that Caroline was known for her beauty. Caroline attended the University of Technology in Lae, but only for a couple of years.

This information has come from Trobriand islanders, but not from the immediate family, so I can't vouch for the exact accuracy of what I have been told. Those I spoke to said what they were telling me is what is generally spoken about and known by the community.

I cried. And for the first time Caroline became real for me. I understood why Wayne had kept Caroline and what he'd done to her a secret. How could anyone find the words to explain the loss of this beautiful young woman?

I'd married a man I judged to be extraordinary. I still perceived him to be extraordinary. But more complicated, more flawed, than I'd ever imagined. Sometimes, the frustration I felt was that this astonishing relationship—which still endured, albeit in a lopsided manner—was going to hobble me for the rest of my life. For as much as I still believed in the importance of understanding your history in order to become complete, I found it impossible to connect Wayne from 1978 with the individual I knew and loved. I consciously tried. I bent and twisted my intellect to the problem. I attempted for hours to push this one version of Wayne into the other. But it was beyond my ability to fuse these two versions of the same man. My heart argued against my principles. I read everything I could on cognitive dissonance—how conflicting beliefs caused people emotional discomfort and that to restore a sense of equilibrium, individuals usually explained one side of the equation away. I knew I didn't want to be that person.

Instead, I constructed an emotional division in my mind. I managed by viewing Wayne as two distinct individuals: the young, rough, barefoot guy who killed his beautiful girlfriend one humid night in Goroka. Either accidentally or on purpose. And then there was the man I knew, who wrapped his arms about me and kept me loved and safe—two opposing ideas held in my mind simultaneously. And I waited to see what New Guinea would tell me.

36

Sydney airport, January 2018

EYES HARDENED, I SLAP MY passport onto the counter and check-in at the Air Niugini counter at Sydney International Airport. 'I have ashes in my carry-on luggage.'

Bathed in bright morning light the woman says, 'Should be fine, but I'll just let Marie know, so she can let Port Moresby know.'

Hat on my head, channelling Indiana Jones, I smile assertively at the security officials in their navy-blue uniforms. Place my phone and my iPad into a separate tray. Step through the body scanner. No red lights! I'm ready to extricate the paperwork from the funeral home, as my backpack trundles through the X-ray machine, but no one is interested.

Downing a coffee standing up, in one of those expensive cafes outside the duty-free shopping area, I successfully ignore the hum of thousands of people milling about under fluorescent lights. Heavy-bellied planes roar as they lift from the runway like oversized pelicans. And suddenly I'm in the lounge, waiting for the flight to be called. My phone buzzes. 'Love you, Mum. Stay safe.' The message from Jonno is the last thing I read before the boarding announcement is made.

Beside me on the plane is an expat who has been living in Port Moresby for two months, on contract for an Australian bank. He thinks he knows it all.

'It's not as bad as everyone says. Just keep the doors locked when you're driving. Don't walk anywhere by yourself. And, certainly, don't go out at night on your own.'

I nod. Try not to say too much, conscious of the limited room between our economy seats and the chicken salad I ate last night at the airport hotel—with its garlic dressing. But the drone of the engine makes it hard to hear everything he says and, despite my judgements about him, I'm still eager to know his impressions. I lean towards him, over the armrest. An announcement is made, barely audible over the drone of the engine: 'Chewing betel nut is banned during the flight.'

'Oh, you'll get used to that,' my new friend says. 'First time I saw it I thought my driver had been in a fight and had been punched in the mouth. It makes everyone look like their tongue—their whole mouth—is bleeding. It's supposed to be illegal but everyone does it.'

I nod again.

He goes on to describe the pristine coastlines. When I mention I'm heading to Rabaul he suggests hiking up the volcano, as long as it's not too active at the moment. 'And you must not miss snorkelling at Kimbo.'

He tells me he brought all his scuba-diving gear with him this trip and he was not even charged for the excess baggage. 'You'll get used to that, too. Expect the unexpected.' I sit back, stare out the little round window. My ears pop. The sea lies below, flat and blue. Silas, too, has mentioned the volcano. And snorkelling. Plus, he is happy to 'drive me down the coast to meet Dad'.

The solid male steward appears in the aisle by my seat row. He is cheerful and unbelievably generous. Three bourbon and Cokes, unasked for by my new friend sitting beside me, are laid on his tray table. After I ask for a gin and tonic, I'm brought a second when the first glass is barely empty, but I can't. I'm too conscious of the looming interaction to come—especially the declaration of the ashes and what kind of reaction there will be at security when I inform them.

But airport security was uneventful. If I'd answered 'no' to the man standing beside the lone bollard indicating New Guinea screening procedures—I would have been waved past the X-ray machines like all the other passengers—who obviously know the drill. As it is, I'm the sole individual with anything to declare and the guard doesn't even ask me to open my bag. But what does it matter? Because I'm on an adventure and I'm in New Guinea and I'm bringing Wayne home.

Robert, Martha's former second husband, picks me up from the hotel, as arranged. I climb into an enormous, mud-spattered Land Rover and meet Wati, his Suva-born wife, and their seventeen-year old-son, Paul, who looks like he should be playing for the Fijian Rugby team. They'd all waved me into the front passenger seat, so I perch forward, peering through the cracked windscreen, impatient to see what Port Moresby is like.

The road is pitted bitumen and the other drivers are reckless, but it is the crowds of local people—parades of them, filing along the roadside—who astound me. So many people. All shifting in single file. All travelling in the same direction. To me it looks like an exodus. Robert indicates the multitudes. 'Price of cars makes them beyond the dreams of most.'

People wear clothes of every colour of the rainbow. Some of

the women walk with the straps of their bags slung around their foreheads. Everyone is forced to make their way across vast, empty paddocks of mud, sometimes with emaciated dogs trotting and sniffing behind them.

Robert steers the car over a steep hill and as we crest the pinnacle, the harbour materialises before us, more splendid than I'd imagined: wide and smooth and clear. The opposite shore is circled by deep green hills, rolling all the way down to the edge of the water. A storm is gathering. The opaque colours of the landscape remind me of the Romantics, of Wordsworth, of an oil painting by Delacroix. Everything is bathed in ethereal golden light. Banks of clouds hang above what appears an endless stretch of metal-coloured harbour.

Tomorrow I fly to Rabaul.

37

East New Britain, January 2018

Friday

I'M ABOUT TO MEET JOHN, here at my hotel. The sky is a broad blue and waves are slapping against the shore only metres away. I'm resting on what feels like the edge of the world. I hear the crunch on the gravel as a four-wheel drive passes through the gates.

A tall man, taller even than Wayne, unfolds from the car—he is rangy and thin. My heart swells so much I think I will choke. It's my husband, but also, it is not. For the first half hour, below slow-circling ceiling fans, we are stiff and formal with each other. But his hands. His arms. His forthright gaze. The complicated sorrow in his golden eyes. In him I see Wayne, and I think I could sit here with my husband's brother forever, simply watching him, listening to him, saying nothing. For what can I speak about to this giant of a man who is so similar to the man I love? What can I say that will possibly matter? I fall in love, just a little, with my husband's brother, and feel an urge to follow him wherever the universe turns. I cry repeatedly. John makes references to 'our Wayne'. When I talk about that morning in Portugal, he exonerates me completely. He says, 'If there was anything wrong with his health, to see beforehand, you and I would have been the ones to know it.'

His Dutch-influenced accent sounds brusquer than my husband's did. John's health, to my untrained eye, seems in a worse state than Wayne's was. His skin is permanently sun-bitten, his teeth poorly maintained, his knuckles and bones stiff. I imagine it is the thirty-five extra years he has spent in the tropics. Twice he says to me, 'Anything you want to know, just ask me.'

But the one question I must have an answer to seems unable to move out of my mouth.

Saturday

John's adult daughter, Rebecca, drives me around the island in a weathered Landcruiser ute, always with several 'boys' sprawled on the back tray. She manages an international business, in partnership with her mother, and is currently attending, by distance education, the University of New England.

Here in East New Britain, she tells me, it is relatively safe—compared to the main island. There are armed hold-ups on the road, apparently, but this young woman is confident and sensible. She pushes the gear stick about with authority. Rides roughshod over potholes. Frankly answers all my questions.

'Yes,' she agrees, 'the torture and killing of women does occur, right here on this island and across PNG, often because of witchcraft allegations. One killing happened last week. The women and girls were burnt with hot sticks, stoned, penetrated with machetes.'

I swallow.

'Yes, the custom of bride price exists.' In fact, if Rebecca is ever to marry, she says, the man will probably have to pay for her. She defends the custom when she sees my shocked face, because, she says, patting her heart, the custom is simply recognising her value.

Yes, her position as an educated woman causes difficulties. Not just in finding a partner. Being a woman who is independent, bi-racial and who wears Western clothing creates hurdles. Over the days I spend with her, Rebecca inspires my deep respect.

Then she tires of the conversation. Points instead to the blue volcano across the soft blue bay, to the tunnels hidden amongst the rocky cliffs, dug by Japanese soldiers during the war. She directs my attention to the lines of fish, hanging on strings from the tree branches, to the local people standing beside them—fanning small fires to smoke the fish in preparation for sale. Half a dozen silver-scaled slips of white meat glint in the sun between the smoke haze and the sea.

Rebecca is driving me up the mountains, to where she lives with her mother, Tammi. John's second wife, Lillian, rides in the back tray with the boys.

'Don't worry about me, Aunty Susan.' Lillian flashes me a big grin as she hauls herself up over the tyre, 'I am used to it.'

With the windows wound down, the air turns cooler as we ride higher. Lillian leans out over the road, twisting her body around the space between the cab and the tray, and shouts through the rushing wind, 'Aunty Susan, this is my village.'

The road is almost empty of people. Coconut and mango and banana trees grow so close to the edge of the track that I can almost reach through the window and pick the fruit. Rebecca pulls the car up at a little wooden stall and buys lady finger bananas. Lillian takes my hand, draws me to the edge of the valley, and the green jungle falls away below me, all the way to the gleaming coast.

On Tammi's plantation there is a small hut about a kilometre away from the main house. John is waiting there to speak with me. I tramp along a narrow track, through guava trees, past durian fruit piled high in the sun, past acres of coconut and avocado trees.

Listen to the clicking of the crickets. The quiet rustle in the trees. Several bone-thin mutts trot beside me. The female has recently birthed a litter and her black protruding teats drag across the undergrowth.

John sits in a rocking chair on the wooden porch. His various kids, adopted and genetic, black and white, are scampering amongst the overgrown grass. They knock the guava down from the branches with a long pole made from bamboo. He is surrounded by tools and rusting pieces of metal and bits from machines. His head is bent. He is fiddling some twine around a knife. There are holes in the wooden floorboards and I can see the dirt below.

John stands and we shake hands formally. He motions to another chair and I sit beside him. We discuss the history of the Highlands, the famous explorers the Leahy brothers, and the experiences he and Wayne shared as young men, driving trucks for Stan. He is, as they say, a man of few words, but he is making an effort for me.

In return, I cannot speak for fear of saying the wrong thing. For fear of sounding foolish. For fear of giving offence. But if I don't ask now, will I ever have the opportunity again? My heart stops beating.

'John?'

He knows what I am going to say. Still, I feel forced to wrap it in a multitude of words. But eventually, 'I will always love your brother. But I need to know what happened that night.'

He turns his head stiffly, draws deep on his cigarette, and nods.

I prompt him. 'You paid for the QC to come up from Brisbane.'

He nods again. Waits, with a world of patience. Stretches his long legs in front of him. Then, he says, 'I spoke about all this business with Silas. He told me what you wanted to ask. I was worried, Suzy. Worried you wouldn't want to hear what I had to say. But Silas said all you want is the truth.'

'When you only know this much of the story,' and I hold up my thumb and forefinger in the air, half an inch of space between, 'then it's too easy to fill in the rest with too much imagination.'

John gazes out over the fruit trees. There is a Japanese cement bunker from WWII, half hidden between the palms, and his attention seems drawn there. He turns his head again to look at me, looks at my fingers, still held in mid-air, and it is Wayne's gaze on my face. Heat prickles on the back of my neck and sweat dribbles down inside the cotton 'meri blouse' I'm wearing.

I say, 'If he stomped on Caroline—I will deal with that. But if she fell, then it would be good to know that, too.'

John leans back in the chair. Rocks. Takes another drag. 'All that business about stomping,' he makes a dismissive wave with his free hand, ' . . . just bullshit.'

I stop breathing. Shift forward.

'I was there two hours before it happened, hey?' He contemplates the cement bunker again. 'Then I had to drive back to Lae. But two of my mates stayed. They were there when it happened. Old bushies. Would never tell a lie. Not to me. Straight as a die, they were.' He rubs his face with his arthritic hands, and it is Wayne again.

Then he turns to me. His face a portrait of truth.

'Caroline was with him at the top of the stairs. He was trying to put the key in the lock. He pushed her off because she was grabbing him around the neck.' John meets my eyes steadily. 'She fell hard, and tumbled right over the side of the banister. She bounced off the railing. She fell all the way down to the very bottom.'

We both sit in silence.

I can hear the workmen round the side of the building, the buzzing of a whipper snipper.

'My brother was always stronger than he knew. But he never

meant to harm Caroline.' John shakes his head. 'It was an accident. Pure and simple.'

I start to cry openly. Wipe my wet face with the back of my hand and stare at the palm trees blowing in the wind.

John pushes a rusting lawnmower part away with his boot. Wedges it against the table holding all manner of metal bits and pieces, a plastic Coke bottle cut in half he uses as a spout, a jumble of things I have no understanding about. He shouts out to a boy down near the bunker in Pidgin. Something about the ratio of petrol and diesel to fill the plastic container.

John's beautiful, tiny daughter, who likes to be called Roseanne when she is speaking in English and Leanne when she is speaking Pidgin, pushes her face through the broken screen door and runs towards us, climbs onto my lap. She begins to click the hoops I am wearing in my ears with her fingers.

John has tears in his eyes and he wipes them away roughly.

'Takes a lot to get water into my eyes,' he says.

'That night was merciless. And both of us, well, we had to put it behind us. To get on. But what he'd done was always there. It never went away.' He raises his eyes to the sky. 'My brother felt terrible guilt and shame about killing Caroline. But the rest of that stuff said in court, about what happened at the bottom of the stairs, that was all bullshit. We're pretty rough and ready people, hey? You can see that. So judge us as you will. But we tell it how it is.'

I nod in gratitude.

'My brother and me? We were like that.' And he raises his hand, first and second finger jammed against each other. There are no gaps between. And in his deep authoritative voice says, 'It was an accident. But one he had to pay for, true enough . . .' He points his gaze at me and smiles, sadly. 'One he paid for the whole of his life.'

38

Goroka, January 2018

THE FUCKING PLANE IS TINY. Pea-sized. It's so little that in a mad panic I think I could push it all the way to Goroka. It's parked on the tarmac, of course, and all the passengers—about twenty of us—have to trudge out there in the murderous heat and clamber up a narrow set of stairs. I was the only Caucasian woman in the domestic terminal, and I am the only woman on this plane. But I remind myself that Wayne is here with me, and for the first time, we are running back towards his past. Not away from it. I have given myself the task on this journey of attaching my husband's early years to his later ones.

The propellers crank up. But before I have time to think about vomiting, the man next to me introduces himself.

'I am Clem. I come from a village outside Goroka.'

I shake his hand.

'I am going back to visit my family—to collect my eight-year-old son, to bring him to Moresby to live with me.'

He stares curiously at me. I recollect myself.

'I am Susan . . .' I'm wary about saying my last name, even

though it is different to the name Wayne was known by when he lived here.

'It is nice to meet you, Susan. I work for the University of New England. You know it?' I nod enthusiastically, because it is where I earned my undergraduate degree. And my Master of Letters. I nod because somewhere I love has been mentioned twice in the past week. The journey passes quickly while we reminisce about Armidale.

After we land at the tin shed that is Goroka airport Clem says, 'I will wait with you, Mrs Susan.' So he stands with me, in the dust and the unbelievable humidity. Twice he leaves, twice he returns through guarded metal gates—the surrounding fence is iced with razor wire—always with a shake of his head. Crowds of local people, on the other side of the barrier, stare and whisper about my white skin, my fair hair, my single status. For the remainder of my journey, I notice such curiosity frequently. And I notice this: people either deny the violence is as bad as the media portray it or they refuse to speak of the danger at all. But everyone I meet, even briefly, attempts to protect me. Their actions speak the truth. I'm never once left on my own outside. Not by day, not by night.

Finally, the car arrives from my motel. On the short drive I see that most of the structures in the town were built in the mid-sixties, constructed from fibro and tin, their advertising signage is faded and peeling from decades in the tropical sun. The roads are dirt. Where there is tar, the potholes have been so extensively excavated that ten trucks could be garaged inside them. Mud lies everywhere and smoke thickens the air from fires people light in the streets.

There is the constant movement of people—hundreds, maybe thousands—along the roadsides. But I hear almost no sound— other than car alarms—I think because I'm so overwhelmed by what I'm seeing around me. And even though the smells are intense—the scent of ripe bananas and pineapple is overwhelmingly sweet—I keep focusing back on the people. Shyly extending their hand in greeting. Smiling big smiles. Holding each other by the arm in the streets. Glaucoma or cataracts blanketing the eyes of the aged. The contrast of yellow dirt against the vibrant reds and greens people wear, and the lush green of the foliage against an angry, storm-laden sky.

In the motel room the first thing I notice is the letter from management:

> Please be advised that the main town water from the Goroka dam is experiencing dirty flow of water supply. This is due to continual rain for the last couple of days flooding the main town supply dam. However, water is treated but is not consumable. We have provided complimentary bottles of water in your room for drinking.

This I had expected. The room is clean and bright, with a veranda overlooking the main street. In the afternoon I sit for hours, watching, over rolls of barbed wire, the human parade below. Wishing that things were different and I could venture forth freely.

39

I'M PANICKING BECAUSE IT'S THE day when I'm supposed to be escorted along the Highlands Highway to release Wayne's ashes, and the security team hasn't arrived. I text Stephanie, while behind reception the hotel employee attempts to contact the protection team. The hotel's own security firm (rivals to the company I secured) criss-cross the polished tiles, backwards and forwards, never letting anyone through the front door without a barrage of questions. Security firms are a lucrative business in New Guinea.

An hour later, Nixon arrives. A local man, my height, with a very white smile and a baton hanging from his belt. He has to ask me three times, such is my anxiety, before I respond that yes, I am Miss Susan. I am ushered out the door into the blinding sun and meet Liam, the manager of the Lae branch and the one who is 'personally driving' me today. Nixon climbs into the back and I try, with little dignity, to haul myself into the front passenger seat. I try not to worry about the fact that I am heading off into the highlands of New Guinea with two men I've never met before.

Within minutes, we leave Goroka behind and the countryside unfolds before us. We're surrounded by distant blue mountain peaks, swathed in cloud, by dense coffee plantations and a jungle of lush green. But again, it is the people walking along the road who make the greatest impression on me.

Liam is an ex-policeman. 'My name was given to me by a Marist brother,' he says. He slows the car many times along the route, to stop and chat with the many and various security patrols that are cruising the highway 'looking for trouble'. Everyone seems to know him. Nixon sits rather placidly in the back seat behind me.

This highway is so narrow that in some places two trucks can barely pass one another. If any tar once existed on the road, it has rotted away, enormous potholes take us minutes to bounce down into, rumble through and burst out from again. The heavy over-growth and foliage are so thick it must be true jungle we're driving through.

We begin to climb and Nixon tells me this is the start of the Daulo Pass. Small minivans scoot past us. 'All the people coming in from the other villages,' Nixon says. Because our vehicle is forced to move so laboriously, I stare in detail at the small roadside stalls, made from bamboo and palm leaves. Here, the local people sell coconuts and sweet potato. Black, hairy pigs root in the undergrowth. Dogs—whose every rib I can count—scrabble in the muck on the verge. Small half-naked infants toddle behind the animals.

Bumping up the mountain, scaling in and out of potholes, I cling to the grab-handle above the window, bracing myself against the jolts. Then, on a steep uphill run, just before a sharp curve in the road, on a dirt straight about two hundred metres long, I see men—an immense pack of swarming men. I see the massive logs they've dragged across the road. There is no way for our ute to go around. It is a roadblock.

I glance to my right. I glance behind me. I stare at the man next to me, behind the wheel; I turn my head and stare at the man seated behind me and I stare at the men beyond the glass, beginning to surround the car. The violence of Wayne's upbringing, the violence of Caroline's shocking death and the violence of New Guinea amalgamate before me. Violence is presented to me plainly, frankly, shamelessly. This is everyone's reality. Now it's mine, too.

Liam stiffens and reduces speed. Events happen in slow motion. I turn my head to him again; I want to shout, 'Why are you slowing down, for God's sake?' My stomach clenches. I swallow hard and remain silent—I watch it all like I am watching someone else's life. I'm acutely aware of everything I see, everything I do.

I think about being dragged from the car by the mob. I imagine being handled, passed above their heads like a package from one man to the next. Hands gripping my arms. My legs. For the very first time in my rather privileged life, I understand what it means to be a woman in physical fear of men.

The manager of the security company I have hired—ex-policeman, local man—winds down the window and scowls at the youths, who start to shift in a tight horde towards his side of the car. Without any words, he drags a silver object from his pocket. The sun glints off it and I recognise—still in slow motion, like I'm swimming in mud—that it's a gun. Steering with one hand, he rests the revolver on the windowsill, very casually. As we crawl closer and he brakes to a stop, I count about fifty men surrounding the truck. They are young, puffed up, aggressive. I glimpse a machete. Solid wooden clubs being ground up and down into the mud. The shouting, the whistling is wild. Each youth has painted black vertical lines down one side of their face and they press around us, peering intently into the car. There is a suggestion of the vehicle being rocked.

The leader approaches and time spins ever more slowly. There is only this moment. Surprised at my own calmness, I remove my sunglasses, fold them with a click into my lap. Sit up straight. Lift my chin. Stare at the youth through the open window. I am me. Me. I will not give in without a fight.

Some of the adolescents, maybe aged seventeen or younger, eye the gun and back away. I watch their eyes quite literally grow wide. But the leader is tougher, older, more abrasive. He and Liam argue. I am not glanced at once. Every eye is on the ex-police officer, levelling the gun across the sill of the open window.

I understand enough Pidgin to realise the gang are demanding a hundred Kina to let us pass. Liam is shouting back. Asking why. Saying how this is illegal. And later, I learn, he is threatening to bring every policeman he knows back up here that night, to burn down every hut in the village.

The mob grow suddenly humble. Heads nod. Of course, of course, they all appear to be saying. Of course, we will let you through. Why would we ever not? What on earth were we thinking? All smiles to the boss. Salutes.

The corruption, the violence, the abuse of power I have heard so much about are a river running both ways.

Two hours later, on the peak of the mountain, near the threshold of the bordering province, I crouch in a field of wavering grass. My husband's ashes rest beside me, nestled among the ferns. For once, my two bodyguards remain in the car.

Before me is the wide, open sky—and blue hills rolling below.

I lay my palms face down on the ground and kneel in the grass, and I think about what John had told me. About the night

Caroline died. I believe John, even though he is Wayne's brother. The power of his words held truth. His account accords with my memories: about Wayne's size and his inability to gauge his own strength.

In my mind I can see the scene at the top of the stairs. I see my husband angry, impatient, desperate to escape the emotion. I see Caroline, hanging onto him and I see, in slow motion, my husband shrugging her off with a massive shake of his shoulder. *Get off me!* She tumbles over the balustrade. All the way to the cement below.

I start to weep.

For a little while in this world, from within our flawed selves, Wayne and I had given each other everything. Exiled from his childhood home, deeply ashamed, Wayne had been displaced. While I believed that I had no place.

He'd been searching for someone to belong to as much as I.

There is no benevolent god.

But there is this—and I glance at the world before me.

We need to grab it now, just for a minute, and control our destiny while we can.

In 2015, my life had burned tinder dry. The gods had practised their scorched earth policies on me. From a place of profound and compounded grief, with little money, no job and no home, I'd asked myself so often in those first few months, what was the point in living? Where was the meaning in my life? I was less certain about my identity than ever before. Who was I?

So, I became. New. From that empty space, I formed myself afresh. Chose my identity. Finally felt authentic. And not many people can say that. The determination to face problems. The courage to discover what had happened in New Guinea. Picking up the remnants of a passion long ago abandoned and committing myself to writing my story; no matter what others might say. Relying on remaining friends and remaining family. Acting on advice from my mum. From Di. And my husband. And my son. Who was I?

This is who I am.

❀

Standing, I consciously forced myself to think of one of my favourite memories—Wayne and I were together on the coast of South Australia. We were on our way home—at last—from Perth. It was 2014.

Our accommodation that night was a room built from besser blocks, attached to the solitary pub in front of us. The building squatted in the middle of nowhere, beside the main highway that cut Australia in half. Under a raw moon, a dingo slunk away from us through the dirt. The engines of several rusted-out vehicles were ditched round the side of the hotel, like mechanical flora.

'I'll go get us booked in. Stay here.' When he left, I'd never heard such silence.

Ten minutes later, I stepped through the doorway of our room, and it was as ghastly as we'd imagined. The mask of bleach almost suffocated me. The double bed was lumpy, covered by a faded chenille bedspread. Dusty, artificial roses had been jammed into a vase on top of the circa 1978 television. We laughed together in the middle of that stale space. Then we kissed. He groaned as he gathered me to him. I slowly submerged within his grip, till he was the only thing holding me upright.

Falling onto the bed, I clutched the sheets between my fingers. He flattened me to the mattress, snatched up my hair and came in a wild, single roar.

Afterwards, I relaxed and smiled, settling into pinnacles of bliss, because it was me who had roused him so. Swinging his leg off me and crashing down flat onto his back, he dragged me in tight, below his shoulder, his arm snaked under and around me, so I fitted in snugly beside him. He couldn't speak. Instead, he expressed his love by intermittently crushing me to him, ever more tightly.

Curling on my side, with my nose pressed into his soft skin, swallowing the peppery smell of him, I lay my hand flat on his belly, listening to his breathing.

Using his native Pidgin, the first word he whispered was 'meri'. He had explained before. It was literally derived from the word 'Mary' and meant significant woman.

'Yu bilong mi meri. Mi laikim yu oltaim.'

As he fell asleep, I curved in beside him.

The following morning, I was as happy as I'd ever be, I knew that, even then.

Wayne was spread out naked across the sheets, snoring, completely relaxed. Drawing my jeans up from where they were still pooled on the floor from last night, dragging on a singlet, I took a few quiet steps to the door and peered out, squinting against the emerging day. Squatting on the cement step, my gaze panning from east to west, I followed the line of the rising sun.

The land was unreservedly free of trees. There were no mountains, or even hills. There were no other buildings. There were no other human beings or living animals. Except for the fat barrel of a blue heeler who came sniffing his way across the dirt, tongue lolling in the growing heat. Wagging his tail lazily and snaking up beside my bare feet on the step, he licked me wetly across my toes. There was a gusty sigh as he settled down.

Laughing in the still air, pressing the soft inside of my upper arm against my mouth to muffle the noise, I scratched the dog between his ears, watching the countryside, amazed at the silence.

Sensing the door crack open behind me, I know Wayne is at my back. He drops a kiss to the top of my head and we go for an early morning stroll along the cliffs above the Bight and stare in wonder at whales breaching so close to shore. That the Great Southern Ocean crashes so close by, so vividly blue, against the dull brown of the Nullarbor Plain behind us, astounds us both. I stick out my tongue, lick salt from the wind; stand with him in the space between desert and sea. He places his substantial hand on my shoulder, turns me towards him against the bluster of the sea gale.

'Promise me we can look forward to the future now, Suz? We've got a year in Spain to plan for, girl. Our own life to live.' And he squeezes me. 'Maybe even a marriage to arrange,' and as I glance up in surprise, he grins at me. 'You know how much I love you.'

To wed him is all I've ever wanted—to be his wife, to be married to this man. Wayne's willingness to always look after my happiness, his commitment to making all my dreams come true, is probably at the core of this new idea. He knows me inside and out. He will marry me, essentially, because he knows it will make me happy. Standing on my toes, I lean up and kiss him full on the mouth as the wind whips about us. He pulls me closer to him, the sea shining below us.

'I love you too, Wayne Francis.'

I hang my arms around his neck, kiss him more deeply, drawing his mouth to mine, a sunny sort of daze engulfing me as it always does when we are one. Then I step back, stare up at his generous face framed against the wide Australian sky.

'All this searching for where I belong in the world? Now that I understand what happened in the past, I think I can finally move forward.'

Wayne gathers my hands in his and we are connected once more.

'Thank you,' I say to him. 'For this moment right now, for everything that has been and for everything that will be.'

And up a mountain in New Guinea, beside his beloved Highlands Highway, I leap into the air and throw my husband's ashes to the sky.

Acknowledgements

Where do I start?

To my wonderful family and friends who supported me after Wayne's death, especially my brother, Pete. I managed to finish this book because every one of you listened endlessly to my anxieties and my doubts, and helped me through the most distressing period of my life. I could not have found happiness again, let alone published a book, without Jonno, Di, Pete, Jan, Liam, Maddison, Siobhan, Geoff, Caitlin, Ashleigh, Christa, Gai, Damien, Trudy and Amelia, and all my friends from Mendooran. A special mention must be given to my sister Mary, who gave me the final piece of the jigsaw. And to the lovely Jaimie, who was there with Jonno when I came home, and bought me pyjamas.

And thanks to Wayne's mum and his extended family, who were always respectful and kind to me, offering shelter, emotional support and practical assistance—like a new key for Wayne's car, when the original could not be found, or the advice I received about where to stay in Port Moresby. You all helped me, perhaps more than you realise, and I hope the book makes you proud.

Wendy James, you are a constant friend and such an inspiration, and your support and endless encouragement drove me forward.

Nor could the book have been achieved without my writers' group—Margaret, Michelle, Hilary, Jamie and Mick—who read early drafts repeatedly, and Annemarie Laurence who first sent my story to ABC Conversations, which was the breakthrough I needed.

To Varuna, the National Writers' House, who have always been so supportive of my writing—I thank you for awarding the original manuscript a final place in the Publishers Introduction Program in 2017. That's when I finally began to believe that my book had merit.

And to Dr Carol Major, who read the manuscript a number of times and offered invaluable advice. You were a bright voice in a difficult world.

Margaret Gee was one of the first people who saw what the book could become, and my gratitude to you knows no bounds.

My thanks also to the *ABC Conversations* crew, especially Nicola Harrison and Sarah Macdonald, who made the radio interview process easy and enjoyable with their compassion and kindness and generosity of spirit.

Of course, the brilliant crew at Allen & Unwin need recognition. Especially Annette Barlow, a great Australian publisher, who took a chance on me. For a debut author, the experience has been made seamless and no question is ever insignificant. Annette inspires great confidence in me, and my appreciation is impossible to express. To Samantha—a calm and wise and careful senior editor who held my hand and offered her time and expertise, guiding me through all stages of the process. Also, to Julia and Alison, editors extraordinaire, my deepest respect. And to the marketing and sales teams—you guys are awesome! Thank you. Here I need to make mention of Christa Moffitt, who designed a book cover so beautiful it made me cry.

I also want to pay special tribute to the best literary agent in the world—Benython Oldfield. Without whom none of this would have happened. You have my eternal respect and my thanks. Words are not enough to express what you have given me.

And there's a special group of people I also need to mention. The strangers who guided me through the nightmare that was Wayne's death: Angela at the consulate (Angela is a pseudonym but she knows who she is), the lovely Toni at my solicitors, and the friends I made in Granada.

Also, Allison and Darren Writer, Wayne's long-time friends whom he loved very much.

Finally, Wayne—a man who loved me unconditionally. You gave me the greatest gift—the one I really needed. I will carry you in my heart forever.

About the Author

Susan Francis lives in a small house in Newcastle, happily alone aside from a family of magpies who regularly call in for a feed. These days she writes full-time, occasionally tutoring HSC students brighter than she cares to admit. She has previously been employed in various occupations: as a high school English teacher, as a proofreader, in advertising, as an enrolled nurse; and she once served Stevie Wright cocktails at an underground bar in Kings Cross. She earned a Master of Letters in Australian literature during the 1990s, while raising her son, Jonno. She has lived in Indonesia, the United Kingdom and Spain, and has travelled widely. She speaks Spanish— and Bahasa Indonesian very, very badly.

An earlier version of *The Love that Remains* was a finalist in the 2017 Publishers Introduction Program, run by Varuna, The National Writer's House in Katoomba. Galvanised by this success, a friend nominated Susan's story for *ABC Conversations*, and her interview with Sarah Macdonald went to air in the same year. Meanwhile, Susan busied herself writing short stories, achieving a measure of success. Then, she struck a deal with her first agent. A round of submissions to publishers ensued, entailing additional work on her manuscript. After a few close calls but no contract, Susan decided to rework her book, adding the third (and final) section. In 2019, her current agent secured a contract for her memoir with Allen & Unwin.

Susan is currently working on her first novel, set between the north coast of NSW, Indonesia and Timor Leste. Inspired by memories of living in Java as an eighteen-year-old, Susan again explores themes of what makes us who we are, the impact of secrets, and the effects of grief and betrayal on our lives. Gin is still her favourite beverage. Books her passion. Photography a valuable hobby. Jonno frequently zooms up the highway from Sydney and advises her to stop worrying about losing weight. Di drops around every week for a cheap Chinese meal. And they keep pretending to each other that one day they will begin walking on a regular basis. By 2021, their friendship will have endured for fifty years.

Susan is once again dreaming about travelling—this time to Balibo.

Wayne remains the man she adores.